D1512317

Quiet Barcelona

Quiet Barcelona

Siobhan Wall
with Cristina Jiménez-Peralta
and Jaume A

FRANCES
LINCOLN

Frances Lincoln Limited
A subsidiary of Quarto Publishing Group UK
74–77 White Lion Street
London N1 9PF

Quiet Barcelona
Copyright © Frances Lincoln Limited 2016
Text © Siobhan Wall
Photographs © Siobhan Wall, Cristina Jiménez-Peralta and Jaume A except:
p.74 Laie, p.93 Grand Hotel Central Barcelona, p.103 Nougueras Blanchard,
p.136 Hotel Miramar, p.140 Casa Camper, p.142 Gran Hotel La Florida

First Frances Lincoln edition 2016

All rights reserved.
No part of this publication may be reproduced, stored in a retrieval system, or
transmitted, in any form, or by any means, electronic, mechanical, photocopying,
recording or otherwise without the prior written permission of the publisher or a
licence permitting restricted copying. In the United Kingdom such licences are issued
by the Copyright Licensing Agency, Barnards Inn, 86 Fetter Lane, London, EC4A 1EN.
A catalogue record for this book is available from the British Library.

978-0-7112-3812-1

Printed and bound in China

1 2 3 4 5 6 7 8 9

COVER Casa Mila, Passeig de Gràcia; BACK COVER Jardin Joan Brossa; p.1 Catedral
Basílica Metropolitana de Barcelona; p.2–3 Sant Pau Recinte Modernista; OPPOSITE
Bunker del Carmel; p.6–7 Passeig de Gràcia; p.8 Casa Vicens; p.9 Bodega La Palma;
p.11 Parc del Laberint d'Horta

Quarto is the authority on a wide range of topics.

Quarto educates, entertains and enriches the lives of
our readers – enthusiasts and lovers of hands-on living.

www.QuartoKnows.com

Contents

Introduction

Barcelona is an enchanting city. With its historic museums, stylish galleries, medieval churches and secret squares, it is a very rewarding place to explore, and there are wonderful discoveries to be made around every corner. However, Barcelona is the fourth most popular tourist destination in Europe and in many ways has become a victim of its own success. So many people flock here to see the ancient Barri Gòtic and Gaudí's Modernista architecture that it can be hard to find peaceful places off the beaten track, and it can often be difficult to get away from the noise of the traffic and the crowds. Nevertheless there are many tempting, tranquil places to be found here, from the rugged concrete bunkers that sit high above the city (page 128) to the serene cloisters in the ancient Pedralbes Monastery (page 20) and the bucolic Parc de les Aigües (page 51).

Barcelona became a world city largely through its maritime industry, which opened it up to entrepreneurs and collectors who in turn promoted art and culture. Funds from the catch and sale of fish led to the installation of street lighting in the Barceloneta district, making it easier for ships to locate the

city on their return, and also enabled the construction of the Torre del Rellotge church tower in 1772. The Poblenou district's prestigious fishing history (boats have been setting sail from the port since the 14th century) is celebrated in the church of Santa del Maria Mar, where you'll find a model of a medieval ship on the altar.

This thriving industry ensured Barcelona soon emerged as a bustling metropolis of commerce and culture, and the city now boasts an extraordinary number of museums and cultural centres dedicated to its documentation – enough to ensure that not all of them are crowded, especially if you venture away from the main tourist routes. Many of the archeological sites that hint at the city's Roman origins (see Plaça del Rei on page 16, for example) are also open to the public thanks to MUHBA (Museu d'Història de Barcelona). The council-funded organisation has been committed to preserving, documenting and studying the city's history since 1943.

The Acadèmia Sant Jordi (page 27) is particularly special, one of just two in Catalunya that have kept their original 19th-century art museum structures. Here you'll find high, sweeping ceilings and walls entirely covered in artworks; diffused lighting falling on the colourful paintwork makes these rooms look like artworks in themselves. Even the Fundació Antoni Tàpies (page 14), a 19th-century industrial building converted into a permanent homage to the Spanish master, is usually empty and peaceful. Of course, Barcelona's art and

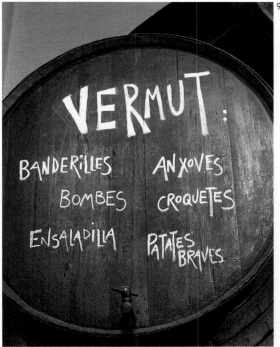

culture scene continues to flourish, as can be seen in the numerous galleries scattered about the city that showcase the very best in both international and Catalan modern art. The prestigious Sala Parés gallery has exhibited industry greats from Picasso to Francesco Goya, while the Nogueras Blanchard gallery works with conceptual artists to initiate some truly groundbreaking projects.

The commercial side of Barcelona's history can also be found in the centenary shops of the gothic quarter. These old-fashioned *botigues* (boutiques) have been around for over 100 years and continue to trade today, thanks to their high-quality products and consistently courteous service. Around 32 of these shops remain, and each of them specialises in one particular product – one of the best things to do in the city is wander through the twisting lanes of this district to seek them out. Cereria Subira (page 73) continues to produce its own hand-dipped and moulded candles, while the quaint Arc Iris in Passeig de Gràcia sells corsets and brassieres. Another highlight is Sombrerería Obach (page 63), a specialist hat and cap shop. The current owner's great-grandfather bought the shop many decades ago and his original fixtures and fittings are still here. With its ticking clock, carved mirrors and wooden cupboards, it's a charming spot to try on a barretina – the traditional Barcelona headgear. If you happen to be a sports fan, you can also get a red and yellow football cap here. As well as being picturesque heritage establishments sporting curved brass door handles and polished wood counters, these shops are also very useful, practical stores where you can purchase everything from garden shears to stationery. La Casa de Les Sabatilles (page 64) is a lovely shop that sells only Spanish-made espadrilles. Try a satin lace pair tied with delicate ankle ribbons or a simple leather sandal. Piled high with shoe boxes, this is a place to treasure.

Perhaps one of the greatest aspects of this popular holiday destination, however – particularly when it comes to seeking peace and quiet – is its climate. Barcelona is an outdoor city, and boasts a huge number of parks, gardens and green spaces. Those in the centre can often get crowded, but slightly further afield lie some exceptionally calm, open spaces. The Botanic Garden (page 39) takes visitors on a tour of Mediterranean climates around the world and the species of plants that live there, while you can lose yourself in an 18th-century topiary maze at the Parc del Laberint d'Horta. Parc de l'Oreneta (page 41) is also an ideal spot for a picnic with spectacular views. Stunning vistas are not in short supply here – Barcelona is bordered by the rolling hills of the Parc Natural de la Serra de Collserola, which offer a whole new perspective on the city and the Mediterranean Sea below. And these views only get better as the sun sets – a climb up Montjuïc Hill in the early evening leads to the garden of the Miramar Hotel (page 137) where visitors can treat themselves to a refreshing drink overlooking the shimmering pool. Aside from the call of crickets, there's very little to distract you from gazing at the stars or watching the ships slowly pull into the harbour below.

Of course we can't speak of Barcelona and not speak of its food. As in many modern cities, finding music-free restaurants isn't easy, but the wealth of cafes and restaurants populating these streets means you're sure to find one. Avoid the clamour of La Rambla and head for local favourites such as Casa Amalia (page 123) next to the Mercat de la Concepio, which serves its delicious, authentic food in unassuming surroundings.

In Spain, the midday meal is more important than an evening supper, so don't be surprised if locals tuck in to what looks like a three-course banquet for lunch. Early evening is in fact one of the quietest times to dine out here. If you're after a quick afternoon snack, head to one of Barcelona's famous *bodegas* (wine cellars) for a slice of *jamón ibérico* (cured ham) and a glass of cava – Bar Bodega Quimet (page 114) is one of a few in the middle of town that has managed to retain some of that traditional Catalan atmosphere. Whether meeting up with friends for a drink in the urban surrounds of Plaça de les Glòries Catalanes (page 134) and Avinguda de Gaudí (page 130), or simply seeking a coffee to enjoy while reading your book, you're sure to find a secret spot of your own if you look hard enough.

Seeking spaces of solitude is at the heart of *Quiet Barcelona*, and this book hopes to start you on your journey of calm discovery in one of the world's busiest cities. Explore stylish galleries, ancient shopping quarters, peaceful places of worship and hushed libraries, or strike out on a long, languorous walk and end with a refreshing dip in the sea. There are numerous ways to appreciate Barcelona's more serene side, and there are many quiet corners to be found in every district of this magnificent, exhilarating city.

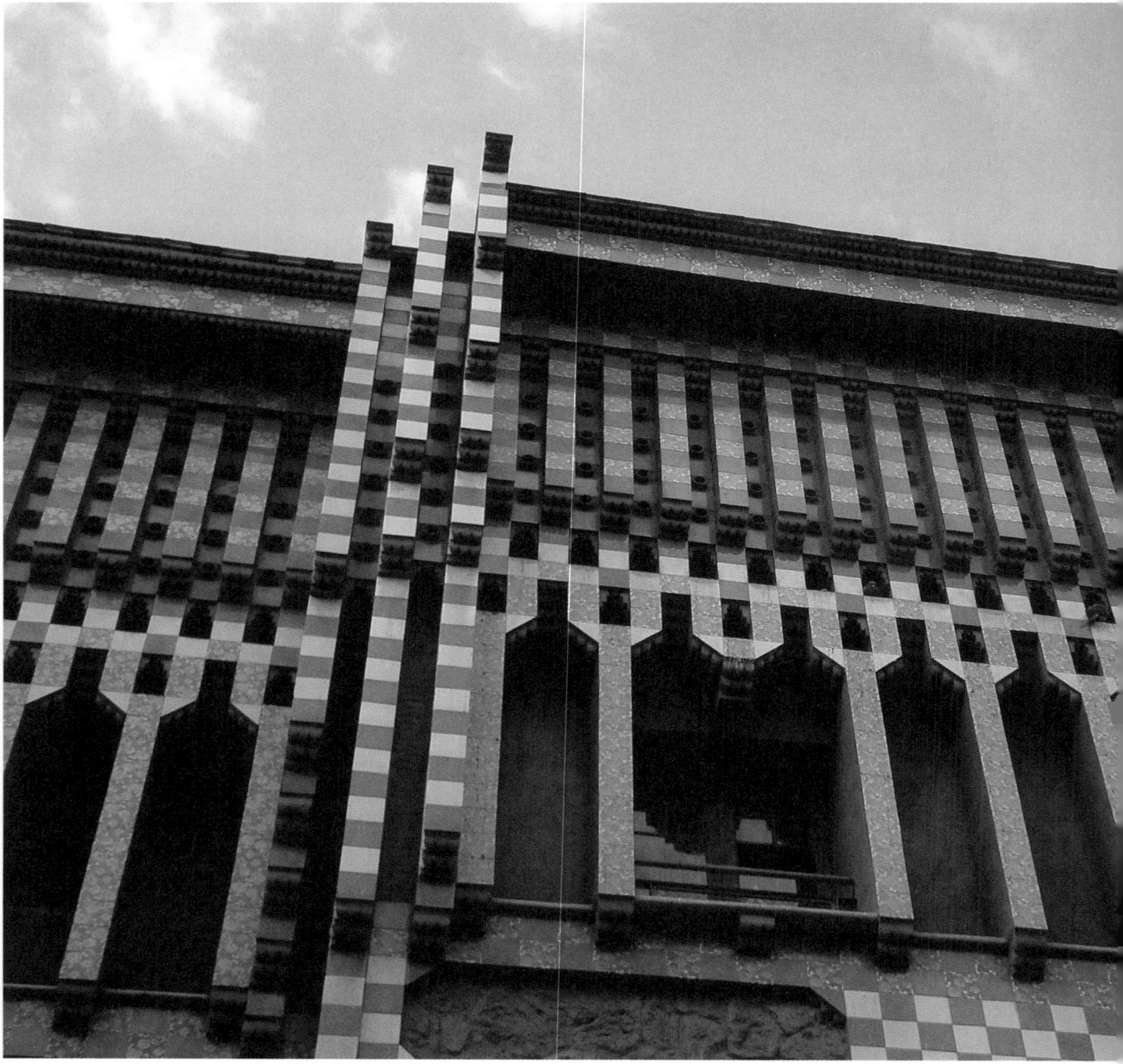

Museums

Casa Vicens

Carrer de les Carolines 18–24, 08012
Free www.casavicens.org
The building itself is closed to the public
but can be viewed from the street
Metro Fontana, Lesseps **Bus** 22, 24, 87, V17
Train Plaça Molina, Sant Gervasi
The surrounding pavements are wheelchair accessible

The very first house Gaudí designed, this is one of the most
striking buildings in the city. Turquoise and white tiles cover the
exterior, along with ornate black ironwork, fairytale turrets and
moulded tiles covered in sunflowers and leaves. Oriel windows
protrude from the walls of the building and the chequerboard
tile effect suggests that Gaudí had a wonderfully irreverent
sense of humour. This is a Unesco World Heritage building, and
it is a vivid, hundred-year-old reminder of the ingenuity and
imagination of Barcelona's most famous resident.

Fundació Antoni Tàpies

Aragó 255, 08007
☎ 934 870 315
€ www.fundaciotapies.org
Open Tuesday–Sunday 10am to 7pm
Metro Passeig de Gràcia **Bus** 7, 20, 22, 24, H10 **Train** Provença
For wheelchair access, ring the doorbell to the left of the main entrance

Antoni Tàpies is renowned for his large, gestural works which include images of huge painted crosses on everyday materials such as sacking, sand, dried glue and varnish. One of Spain's greatest artists, his semi-abstract paintings still exert considerable influence. There are no permanent exhibits here, but temporary hangings of work by Tàpies and other artists are regularly on display. It is also worth visiting the excellent library which has a world-class collection of books and documents on abstract expressionism and modern art. On the ground floor don't forget to visit the bookshop, which has postcards and other gift items such as tea towels and cotton bags.

Museu Can Framis

Carrer de Roc Boronat 116, 08018 ☎ 933 208 736
€ www.fundaciovilacasas.com
Open Tuesday–Saturday 11am–6pm, Sunday 11am–2pm
Metro Glòries, Llacuna, Poble Nou **Bus** 6, 7, 40, 42, 56,
141, 192, B25 **Tram** Glòries
The museum is wheelchair accessible

Opened by the Vila Casas Foundation in 2009, this
beautifully redesigned art centre is devoted to the display
of contemporary Catalan painting. At any one time you
will see around 300 works of art, dating from the 1960s
to the present day, and all produced by artists who were
born or lived in Catalunya.

Museu d'Història de Catalunya

Plaça de Pau Via 3, 08003 ☎ 932 254 700 or 935 547 427
€ www.mhcat.cat
Open Tuesday, Thursday–Saturday 10am–7pm,
Wednesday 10am–8pm, Sunday 10am–2.30pm
Metro Barceloneta **Bus** 14, 39, 45, 51, 59, 64, D20, H14
The museum is wheelchair accessible

The permanent collection at this museum offers
a comprehensive account of Catalan history from
prehistoric times to the present day. The library is also
an excellent place to study, and is much quieter than the
museum. Avoid the rooftop summer jazz concerts after
dark as these events can get crowded.

MUHBA Plaça del Rei

Plaça del Rei, 08002
☎ 932 562 100
€ (Free on the first Sunday of the month)
www.museuhistoria.bcn.cat
Open Hours vary, check website for details
Metro Catalunya, Jaume I, Liceu, Urquinaona
Bus 45, V15 , V17
The museum is wheelchair accessible

There are number of MUHBA (Museu d´Història de Barcelona) sites around the city, one of which is the ancient city that now lies underneath Plaça del Rei, built by the Romans in the 1st century BC. You can discover the remains of various buildings here, including a laundry, a dyeing workshop and a fish salting factory. One ticket gives access to numerous MUHBA sites of historical significance, including The Door of the Sea – the largest of four entrance gates that, together with 76 imposing watchtowers, formed the city's magnificent defence structure.

Sant Pau Recinte Modernista

Carrer de Sant Antoni Maria Claret 167, 08025 ☎ 935 537 801
€ (Free on the first Sunday of the month) www.santpaubarcelona.org
Open November–March Monday–Saturday 10am–4.30pm, Sunday 10am–2.30pm; April–October Monday–Saturday 10am–6.30pm, Sunday 10am–2.30pm
Metro Dos de Maig, Sant Pau **Bus** 19, 20, 45, 47, 50, 51, 92, 117, 192, H8
The site is wheelchair accessible.

Lluís Domènech i Montaner may not be as well known as the other great Catalan architect, Gaudí, but he nevertheless had a huge influence on the Catalan art nouveau movement. Sant Pau, the world's largest art nouveau site, represents some of his greatest work. The extraordinary collection of buildings was built in the early 1900s as an expansion of Santa Creu hospital, one of the oldest medical institutions in Europe. Medical services ceased here in 2009, but the dramatic masonry and intricate mosaic work have found a new lease of life as a public museum and exhibition space. A guided visit offers a glimpse into the site's history and its enduring artistic merit.

Col-lecció de Carrosses Fúnebres

in Montjuïc Cemetery, Mare de Déu de Port 56–58, 08038

☎ 934 841 999

Free www.cbsa.cat

Open Museum Saturday–Sunday 10am–2pm; cemetery daily 8am–6pm

Bus 21, 107

The museum is wheelchair accessible

Montjuïc Cemetery is not only a lovely place to wander early in the morning as the songbirds stir, it also houses one of the finest collections of funeral carriages and hearses worldwide. Many are over 100 years old and have ornate carvings only found on royal carriages. Draped in black velvet with golden tassels or carrying sombre angels with uplifted arms, these vehicles are fascinating. Some of the carriages are still used, especially during annual parades, and the display is also open during the annual Night of the Museums. It can get quite busy at this time however, so it is best to drop by on a quiet weekend to appreciate the fine craftsmanship and gilded detailing.

Museu d'Idees i Invents de Barcelona (MIBA)

Carrer de la Ciutat 7, 08002 ☎ 933 327 930
€ www.mibamuseum.com
Open Tuesday–Friday 10am–2pm and 4pm–7pm,
Saturday 10am–8pm, Sunday 10am–2pm
Metro Jaume I, Liceu **Bus** 17, 19, 40, 45, 120
The museum is wheelchair accessible

This fascinating museum has an enticing catchphrase:
'Follow our guides into the future.' The unusual
building is full of interactive exhibits, all geared towards
the demonstration and celebration of scientific and
technological innovation. It's a relatively small space,
but thankfully never gets too crowded.

Museu Egipci de Barcelona

Carrer València 284, 08007 ☎ 934 880 188
€ www.museuegipci.com
Open Winter Monday–Friday 10am–2pm and 4pm–8pm,
Saturday 10am–8pm, Sunday 10am–2pm; summer
Monday–Saturday 10am–8pm, Sunday 10am–2pm
Metro Girona, Passeig de Gràcia **Bus** 22, 24, 39, 45, 47
The museum is wheelchair accessible

This private collection of significant Egyptian artefacts
was put together by Jordi Clos, a wealthy hotelier.
Situated in an upmarket area of the city, it's a lovely
escape from the crowds. On sunny days you can also
grab a coffee or tea on the rear terrace.

Reial Monestir de Santa Maria de Pedralbes

Baixada del Monestir 9, 08034
☎ 932 563 434
€ (Free on the first Sunday of the month)
monestirpedralbes.bcn.cat
Open October–March Tuesday–Friday 10am–2pm, Saturday–Sunday 10am–5pm; April–September Tuesday–Friday 10am–5pm, Saturday 10am–7pm, Sunday 10am–8pm
Metro Maria Cristina, Palau Reial **Bus** 63, 78, H4
Train Reina Elisenda
There is partial wheelchair access to the museum and cloisters

This peaceful monastery presents some of the best examples of Catalan gothic architecture in the city. Founded by Queen Elisenda de Montcada in 1327, it housed the Poor Clare Nuns, the female branch of the Franciscan order, and a small group of them continue to live in the adjoining convent today. You can visit the simple unadorned cells where the nuns slept and prayed, as well as the tomb of Queen Elisanda in the church. Other highlights include the extraordinary 14th-century murals in the Abbey room, the early stained glass windows in the Chapter House and the idyllic cloistered garden. The cloister itself is perhaps the most beautiful remaining example of its kind in Europe.

MUHBA Temple d'August

Carrer Paradís 10, 08002 ☎ 932 562 122
Free www.museuhistoria.bcn.cat
Open Monday 10am–2pm, Tuesday–Saturday 10am–7pm,
Sunday 10am–8pm
Metro Catalunya, Jaume I, Liceu **Bus** 14, 59, 45, 64, 120
The pillars can be viewed from the street

Tucked inside an early 20th-century courtyard stand four
nine-metre-high stone pillars – remants of a 2,000-year-
old Roman temple. Most likely built during the reign of
Tiberius, it is incredible that they have survived all these
years. The carved columns with their Corinthian capitals
are an enduring reminder of this city's ancient roots.

Palau Requesens

in the Reial Acadèmia de les Bones Lletres,
Carrer Bisbe Cassador 3, 08002 ☎ 933 270 125
€ www.palaurequesens.cat
Open Guided tours take place on Fridays and Saturdays
from 7.30pm–9.45pm (advance reservation required)
Metro Jaume I **Bus** 45, 120, V15, V17
The building is not wheelchair accessible

The gothic arches and medieval stone balustrades of
this 13th-century palace are simply magnificent. Only the
courtyard is open to visitors, but you can book a guided
tour (available in Spanish and Catalan) to learn about local
Sefarad (Sephardic Jewish) history throughout the ages.

MUHBA Via Sepulcral Romana
Plaça de la Villa de Madrid, 08002 ☎ 932 562 122
€ www.museuhistoria.bcn.cat
Open Tuesday, Thursday 11am–2pm,
Saturday–Sunday 11am to 7pm
Metro Catalunya, Jaume I, Liceu **Bus** 14, 59, 45, 64,120,
The courtyard is wheelchair accessible

In the centre of Barcelona lies a surprising monument
to the city's origins: a collection of 70 Roman tombs.
Unearthed during building work in the 1950s, this
subterranean necropolis now belongs to the MUHBA
(Museu d'Història de Barcelona) and visitors can descend
into the courtyard and wander among the tombs.

Observatori Fabra
Camí de l'Observatori, 08035 ☎ 934 175 736
€ www.fabra.cat
Open Guided tours Sunday 11am, 12.30pm and on
Friday and Saturday evenings between October and
June (advance reservation required)
Bus 111 and a steep walk
The observatory is wheelchair accessible

Visit the observatory after dark and as long as the sky
is clear you will have a spectacular view of the cosmos.
Astronomers give talks and invite you to look through the
oldest telescope ever built. During the summer months
you can also book a table to enjoy dinner under the stars.

Museu Frederic Marès

Plaça Sant Lu 5, 08002
☎ 932 563 500
€ www.museumares.bcn.cat
Open Tuesday–Saturday 10am–7pm, Sunday 11am–8pm
Metro Jaume I, Liceu **Bus** 45, V17
Aside from the basement and the 5th floor, the museum is wheelchair accessible

The sculptor and collector Frederic Marès lived in this grand Catalan house and filled it with historical Hispanic sculpture and fine art. The museum has some outstanding early medieval art, from 14th-century polychrome religious statues to steel helmets worn by indomitable knights. There are also some more recent exhibits, such as 19th-century hand-painted fans and some haunting daguerreotypes in the Collector's Cabinet. Guided tours can be arranged for anyone who is curious about the stories behind the artefacts on display.

Museu del Disseny de Barcelona

Plaça de les Glòries Catalanes 37-38, 08018
☎ 932 566 800
€ www.ajuntament.barcelona.cat/museudeldisseny
Open Tuesday–Sunday 10am–8pm
Metro or **Tram** Glòries **Bus** 7, 60, 92, 192, H12
The museum is wheelchair accessible and wheelchairs are available to hire

The Design Museum in Barcelona is famous for its collection of Catalan-crafted furniture and other fascinating historical ephemera. Some of the most interesting displays can be found in the textile and fashion rooms, where you'll see printed cotton dresses from the 19th century and 1920s beaded, silk crepe georgette tunics. Elsewhere you'll find ceramics painted by Picasso, old wooden blocks used to make hand-printed wallpaper and examples of Catalan graphic design throughout history. If you don't have time to venture inside, the unusual exterior on its own is worth a quick trip. Ring in advance to check when the museum is at its most quiet, as school parties often visit en masse.

Mies van der Rohe Pavilion

Avinguda Francesc Ferrer i Guàrdia 7, 08038

☎ 934 234 016

€ www.miesbcn.com

Open November–February daily 10am–6pm; March–October daily 10am–8pm

Metro or **Train** Plaça Espanya **Bus** 13, 150

The site is wheelchair accessible

The simple, modernist aesthetic of the Mies van der Rohe Pavilion stands in stark contrast to Barcelona's winding medieval streets below. Designed by one of the 20th century's greatest architects, it is a bright, living artwork made of concrete, glass, air and sky; wandering through it you will quickly see that not only are the walls important, but also the spaces between them. The iconic building is also impressive when viewed from the edge of the nearby magic fountain, where you can sit in quiet contemplation. It doesn't take long to explore, so you will also have plenty of time to browse through books on the pavilion in the quiet bookshop next door.

Libraries and cultural centres

Reial Acadèmia Catalana de Belles Arts de Sant Jordi

Passeig d'Isabel II 1, 08003

☎ 933 192 432

Free (Fee for membership, residents only)

www.racba.org

Open Monday–Friday 10am–2pm, closed in August

Metro Barceloneta, Jaume I **Bus** 14, 45, 59, 120, V15 H14

The library is wheelchair accessible but there are no adapted toilet facilities

For a very long time, this magnificent building was home to the Free School of Design, a drawing academy that offered free tuition to aspiring architects and artists (Pablo Picasso among them). In 1989, the non-profit cultural institution was renamed the Catalan Royal Academy of Fine Arts of Sant Jordi to recognise its role as a bastion of the arts in Catalunya. Having separated from the art school, nowadays the aim of the Royal Academy is to preserve, study and make available to scholars the fruits of its rich artistic heritage. The library has been built up through donations and is open to anyone interested in what is a rather idiosyncratic collection of books on the visual arts.

Academia Taure

Carrer d'Astúries 59, 08012 ☎ 932 185 257
€ www.academiataure.com
Open Monday–Friday 11am–1pm and 5pm–9pm, Saturday 10am–2pm (most classes last around two hours)
Metro Fontana, Lesseps **Bus** 22, 24, 39, 114
The academy is not wheelchair accessible

This private academy is over 150 years old and has been inspiring students to learn new skills for over four decades. Book into a class and develop your drawing skills or rediscover old talents; the teachers are enthusiastic and friendly, and always on hand to offer vaulable advice, particlarly if you are new to life drawing. If you've ever dreamt of inventing your own superhero, you can also join the lively Saturday morning class on writing and illustrating comic books.

Biblioteca Sant Pau-Santa Creu

Carrer de l'Hospital 56, 08001 ☎ 933 020 797
Free (Fee for membership, residents only) www.bcn.cat
Open Monday, Wednesday, Friday 3.30pm–8.30pm, Tuesday, Thursday 10am–2pm and 3.30pm–8.30pm, Saturday 10am–2pm **Metro** Liceu, Plaça Catalunya, Sant Antoni **Bus** 59, 91, 120
The library is wheelchair accessible

This wonderful gothic building houses an extraordinary library. Walk up the ancient stone steps to discover a medieval building full of books, DVDs and journals. This ancient biblioteca was a hospice from the 10th century but most of the former hospital was built 400 years later. A public library, it is now open to everyone who lives in Barcelona. It has over 56,000 titles as well as a selection of mainly Catalan and Spanish newspapers and magazines. Cultural activities and book groups are held here as well as activities which encourage children to read. In winter it tends to be quieter, when the square outside is empty and the library windows are more likely to be closed.

Palau Robert Centre d'Informació de Catalunya

Passeig de Gràcia 107, 08008
☎ 932 388 091
Free www.palaurobert.gencat.cat
Open Monday–Saturday 10am–8pm, Sunday 10am–2.30pm
Metro Diagonal **Bus** 6, 33, 22, 24, 34, H8, V17
The centre is wheelchair accessible

Despite being next door to the Office of Tourism on one of the busiest streets in the city, the Palau Robert Information Centre has a surprisingly serene exhibition space. The shows here mainly focus on contemporary photography by Catalan artists so it's a good spot to discover some local talent. Behind the gallery space is a garden with some unusual species of plants and a second exhibition space, housed in some former garage buildings. After a leisurely wander through the centre, pick up a catalogue from the shop; not only a lovely collection of beautiful photographs, it will also serve as a reminder of your trip.

La Virreina Centre de la Imatge

Palau de la Virreina, La Rambla 99, 08002

☎ 933 161 000

Free www.barcelona.cat/lavirreina

Open Tuesday–Sunday and public holidays midday–8pm

Metro Liceu **Bus** 14, 59, 91 **Train** Plaça Catalunya

There is wheelchair access to the first floor exhibition space and adapted toilet facilities

The beautiful Virreina Palace was built between 1772 and 1777 and is one of the most distinctive public buildings in Barcelona. Situated on the famous La Rambla, today it is the headquarters of the city council's Cultural Institute and the first-floor Image Centre hosts a range of temporary art exhibitions and cultural activities. Its programme includes photographic and audiovisual art exhibitions featuring work by both Catalan and international artists, as well as literary festivals, talks and numerous other events, usually connected with ideas surrounding 'the age of the image'.

Centre Cultural La Casa Elizalde

Carrer de València 302, 08009 ☎ 934 880 590
Free (Fee for concerts and courses)
www.casaelizalde.com **Open** Monday–Thursday 9am–
9pm, Friday–Saturday 9am–2pm and 4pm–9pm
Metro Diagonal, Passeig de Gràcia **Bus** 20, 39, 45, 47, H10
Most of the centre is wheelchair accessible

This charming, council-funded space supports a regular
rotation of cultural exhibitions, from photography shows
to music and art discussions, and often showcases works
by Spanish artists rarely seen elsewhere. Ligia Unanue's
intricate geometric sculptures (pictured above) offered a
striking contrast to the dark interior decor.

Fundació Suñol

Passeig de Gràcia 98, 08008 ☎ 934 961 032
€ www.fundaciosunol.org
Open Monday–Friday 11am–2pm and 4pm–8pm,
Saturday 4pm–8pm
Metro Diagonal **Bus** 6, 33, 44, H8, V17
The building is wheelchair accesible

The private art collection of wealthy Catalan lawyer,
journalist and politician Josep Suñol is nothing short of
astonishing, and luckily it's available here for all to see. A
world-renowned archive of 1,200 works includes pieces by
Andy Warhol, Salvador Dalí and Man Ray as well as more
contemporary artists, all with a focus on the avant garde.

Goethe-Institut Barcelona

Carrer Roger de Flor 224, 08025 ☎ 932 926 006
Free (Fee for membership) www.goethe.de
Open Institute Monday–Thursday 9am–2pm and 4pm–8pm, Friday 9am–2pm and 5pm–8pm; library Monday, Wednesday, Friday 10am–2pm and 4pm–8pm, Tuesday 4pm–8pm, Thursday 10am–2pm, closed from late June to late September
Metro Sagrada Familia, Verdaguer **Bus** 19, 33, 34, 50, 51, B24, H10
There is good wheelchair access to the cafe and the library via the entrance on Provenza, 388

Whether or not you are enrolled on a course here, this is a great cultural centre – and not just for Germanophiles. The well-stocked library is a light, spacious room at the back of the building and here you will find everything you need on German literature, arts, music and history. The cafe next door is also lovely. As well as orange juice, organic lemonade, German pilsner and Fritz cola you can order traditional German coffee and cake. The chocolate marble 'kuchen' is especially tempting. With its simple decor and monochrome colour scheme, this is a hidden minimalist architectural gem in a less well-known part of the city.

Arts Santa Mònica

La Rambla 7, 08002 ☎ 935 671 110
Free (Fee for performances)
www.artssantamonica.gencat.cat
Open Tuesday–Saturday 11am–9pm, Sunday 11am–5pm
Metro Drassanes **Bus** 14, 59, 64, 91, 120, D20, H14, N0, N6, N9, N12, N15
The centre is wheelchair accesible

Walking into this beautifully renovated old building at the bottom of La Rambla always feels quietly exciting. As well as ambitious exhibitions of contemporary art, music and literature, numerous other cultural events take place here, in what is a truly impressive space. Attend a Catalan poetry reading in the cloister, meet undiscovered Spanish writers at a literature conference, join in a dance workshop, or watch independent films during an animation festival. The range of creative disciplines on display here is enormously diverse, and a visit is always rewarding.

Biblioteca Jacques Dupin

at Fondació Joan Miro, Parc de Montjuïc, 08038
☎ 934 439 470
Free (Fee for access to the museum)
Open Library Tuesday–Friday 10am–2pm
and 3pm–6pm, Monday, Saturday 10am–2pm;
Museum November–March Tuesday,
Wednesday, Friday 10am–6pm, Thursday
10am–9pm, Saturday 10am–8pm,
April–October Tuesday, Wednesday,
Friday 10am–8pm, Thursday 10am–9pm,
Saturday 10am–8pm
Metro Paral-lel then Funicular de Montjuïc
Bus 55, 150
The building is wheelchair acccesible

The Jacques Dupin Library is without a doubt
the quietest part of the Fundació Joan Miró.
The popularity of this world-renowned Catalan
artist's work can make the main gallery rooms
seem rather crowded, but the library is always
calm. With over 25,000 books and monographs
on the artist and his contemporaries (many
donated by Miró himself), this is an excellent
place to research 20th-century Spanish
modernism. The library doesn't confine itself to
modernist aesthetics, however. It also has an
excellent collection of publications, DVDs and
other materials on art from the 21st century. If
you want to find a truly tranquil spot, walk up
to the roof and bask in the sunshine. Or head
to the peaceful gallery on the upper floor that
displays Joan Miró's own prints, collages and
other works.

Convent dels Àngels

Plaça dels Àngels 1, 08001 ☎ 934 817 922
Free www.macba.cat
Open See website for exhibition details
Metro Bogatell, Ciutadella Villa Olímpica **Bus** 36, 59, H16
The building complex is wheelchair accessible

Since 1999, this convent complex has been home to FAD
(Foment de les Arts i del Disseny), Barcelona's century-old
institute for the promotion and study of contemporary art,
architecture and design. In 2005, part of the convent was
converted to form the MACBA (Museu d'Art Contemporani
de Barcelona) Study Centre, and the chapel is now used as
a venue for occasional exhibitions and concerts.

Dipòsit de les Aigües

Universitat Pompeu Fabra, Campus de la Ciutadella,
Carrer de Ramon Trias Fargas 25–27, 08005
☎ 935 422 000 **Free** www.upf.edu
Open Daily 9am–1pm
Metro Ciutadella Villa Olímpica **Bus** 36, 92, H16, V21, V27
The library is wheelchair accessible

Previously a water tower, fire station and psychiatric
asylum, this adaptable edifice is now one of the libraries
for the Pompeu Fabra University. A quiet place to study,
it's home to the Haas Library and documents from the
Barcelona Chamber of Commerce, making it an
especially unique resource for economic historians.

El Born Centre de Cultura i Memòria

Plaça Comercial 12, 08003 ☎ 932 566 851
Free (Fee for access to the exhibitions)
www.elbornculturaimemoria.barcelona.cat
Open March–September Tuesday–Sunday 10am–8pm; October–February Tuesday–Saturday 10am–7pm, Sunday 10am–8pm
Metro Barceloneta, Jaume I **Bus** 14, 17, 19. 39, 40, 45, 51, 120 **Train** Arc de Triomf, Estació de França
The centre is wheelchair accessible

Book a tour around the El Born Centre for Culture and Memory and you will come to understand how archaeological remains give us extraordinary insight into the workings of the modern-day city. Discover what life was like in Barcelona in 1700, and how different – or similar – it was to the life of the people living here today. After walking around the museum, you can follow the guided tour around the El Born district, an equally fascinating way to learn how the past interacts with the present in this historic quarter of Barcelona.

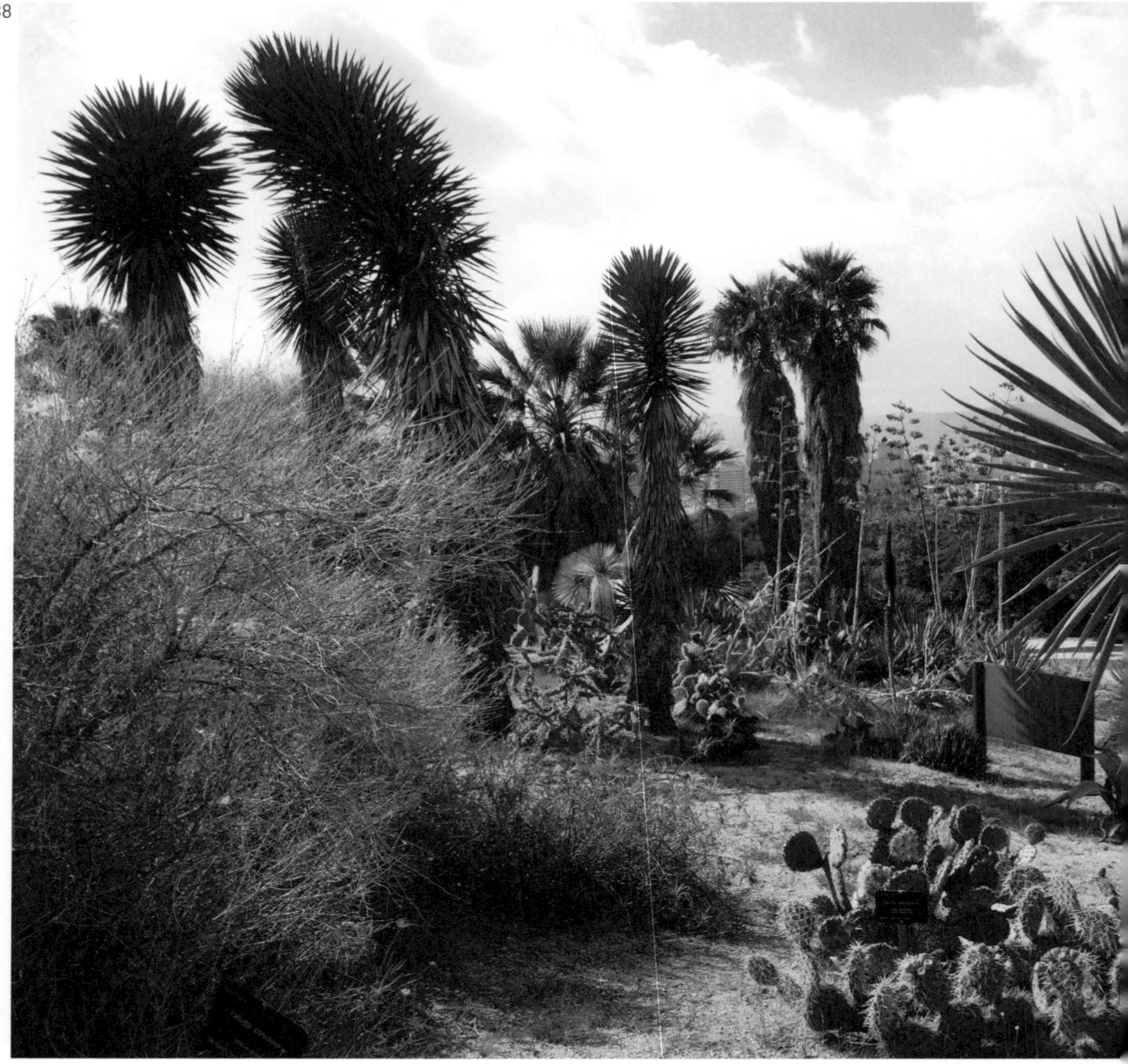

Parks and gardens

Jardí Botànic de Barcelona

Carrer del Doctor Font i Quer 2, 08038
☎ 932 564 160
€ (Free on the first Sunday of the month)
www.museuciencies.cat/en/visitans/jardi-botanic
Open October–March Monday–Sunday 10am–5pm; April–
September Monday–Sunday 10am–7pm
Metro Plaça Espanya **Bus** 13, 150
The garden and cafe are wheelchair accessible

Located high on Montjuïc Hill, Barcelona's botanical garden
contains a diverse array of flora and fauna from various regions
around the world with a climate similar to the Mediterranean.
Visitors can walk through areas filled with plants from South
Africa, Chile, California and Australia, including palm trees,
eucalyptus, stone pines, cacti and fig trees. The wide paths
are easily accessible and zigzag through the site; if you amble
slowly, it can take hours to get around. It's even worth coming
here in inclement weather to visit the Cabinet of Curiosities
at the top of the garden, which is full of unusual natural
specimens, and which offers a glimpse into the history of plant
gathering. If you book a trip in advance, you can also attend
workshops in bonsai pruning and basket weaving.

Carretera de les Aigües

in Parc de Collserola, Carretera de l'Església 92, 08017

☎ 932 803 552

Free www.barcelonaturisme.com

Open All day, every day

Bus 111, 118, 119, 124, 130

Most of the walk is flat so may be accessible for wheelchair users

If you want to explore the hills above Barcelona, there's no better way to do so than by taking a leisurely walk or riding a bike along the Carretera de les Aigües. Local people walk this route often, not only for the mountain air but also for the incredible views all along the path from Sànt Pere Màrtir to the Carretera de l'Arrabassada, and from the Collserola Ridge. The Carretera de les Aigües is named after the water pipes that used to run along its path, and most of the route is still relatively flat. At its highest point, you can look down on the city from 450 metres above sea level.

Parc de l'Oreneta

Carrer de Montevideo 45, 08034
Free www.barcelonaturisme.com
Open December–February daily 10am–6pm;
March and November daily 10am to 7pm; April
and October daily 10am–8pm; May–September
daily 10am–9pm
Bus 60, 66, 130, V3 **Train** Reina Elisenda
Wheelchair access is limited due to steep hills

This lovely park opened at the end of the 1970s
and offers some magnificent views over the city.
Part of the Collserola Ridge, it used to be two
rural estates, one of which was Oreneta Castle,
after which the park is named. Only a few walls
of the ruined castle remain today, however. The
park is full of evergreen and deciduous trees,
including northern red oaks, eucalyptus, pine
and carob, and fruiting cacti. There are lots of
winding paths through woodland, so it's easy to
imagine you are far away from the city. There are
a few designated children's play areas, but away
from these the park can be very peaceful.

Parc de la Creueta del Coll

Passeig de la Mare de Déu del Coll 77, 08023
Free www.barcelonaturisme.com
Open December–February daily 10am–6pm;
March and November 10am–7pm; April and
October daily 10am–8pm; May–September daily
10am–9pm
Metro El Coll La Teixonera **Bus** 87, 92, 119, 129
The area around the pond is wheelchair
accessible but the hills may be difficult to climb

This park is ideal for a scenic wander through
a wooded landscape. High above the city the
Parc de la Crueta del Coll feels wild and full of
rambling plants. In contrast to the more formal
gardens in the city, this is a place where nature
has the upper hand. In among the trees bloom
mauve lobelias and vivid crimson bougainvillea.
The swimming pool, ping-pong tables and other
popular areas are best avoided, but there are
plenty more forested areas to get lost in – be
sure to bring stout shoes or walking boots. On
your way down from the summit of the hill, look
out for the dramatic, concrete claw-shaped
sculpture by Eduardo Chillida, *In Praise of
Water*, that hangs above the pool.

Jardins de Joan Brossa

Plaça de Dante 9999, 08038
Free www.barcelona.cat
Open Daily 10am–sunset
Bus 55, 150, Funicular de Montjuïc
The gardens are wheelchair accessible but the climb up the hill is very steep

Escape the crowds and noise on La Rambla and climb up the steep Avinguda Miramar for a little peace and quiet. At the top of the hill sits this pleasant garden – look out for the statue of the clown Charlie Rivel balancing a ladderback chair on his nose, as well as the sculpture of celebrated 20th-century entertainer Charlie Chaplin. The nearby hills are densely wooded and the paths often feel both close to yet concealed from the city. At dusk you can hear owls among the trees and see lithe bats swooping and diving in the darkening sky.

Jardins de la Vil·la Amèlia

Eduardo Conde 22, 08034
Free www.lameva.barcelona.cat
Open Daily 10am–10.30pm
Metro Maria Cristina **Bus** 130, V3 **Train** Reina Elisanda
The garden is wheelchair accessible

These pretty city gardens have numerous winding paths to stroll down and an enticing variety of trees and flowers in well-kept borders – in spring, locals flock here to catch a glimpse of the pale pink cherry blossom. Further inside the park is a small circular pond which has an island in the centre full of tall grasses, out of which emerges a copper sculpture of a voluptuous naked woman. Created by 19th-century property developer Ignasi Girona in honour of his wife Amelia, it is a quintessential Catalan garden, combining both Northern European and Mediterranean plant species. An outdoor coffee stand with a few chairs provides an unshaded spot to have a drink.

Plaça de l'Ictíneo
Carrer de L'Ictíneo, 08039
Free www.barcelona.callejero.net/placa-de-loctineo
Open All day, every day
Metro Barceloneta **Bus** 45, 59, D20, H14, V17
The gardens are wheelchair accessible

With their neat grassy lawns touched by a gentle sea
breeze, these gardens come highly recommended by
locals as a calm place to relax and recuperate. Ignore the
Moll D'Espanya shopping centre and aquarium nearby
and find a quiet spot here to recline on the grass and read
your book, or take a nap after a long day of sightseeing or
a hard day at work.

Parc Güell
Carrer d'Olot, 08024 ☎ 902 200 302 **Free** (Fee for access
to the Monumental Zone and the Gaudí House Museum)
www.parkguell.cat **Open** Park all day, every day;
Monumental Zone check website for details
Metro Valcarca, Lesseps **Bus** 24, 32, 92, H6
No access for wheelchair users

Despite its popularity, there remain a number of quiet
corners in Antoni Gaudí's famous park. Designed in 1900
for long term friend Eusebi Güell, a wealthy Catalan
entrepreneur, it was used by Gaudí as an opportunity to
make some of the most inventive, unusual sculptures
ever seen in a public space.

Parc del Laberint d'Horta

Passeig dels Castanyers 1, 08035
€ www.barcelonaturisme.com
Open November–February daily 10am–6pm; March and October daily 10am–7pm;
April daily 10am–8pm; May–September daily 10am–9pm
Metro Mundet **Bus** 27, 60, 73, 76, B19
Wheelchair access is limited

Located north of the city close to the university, this park is well-loved by locals. It has a large cypress tree labyrinth in which you can easily lose yourself, or perhaps you'd prefer to be guided by friends as they look down from the handsome 18th-century terrace above. A peaceful location, the park is a mixture of neoclassical pavilions, stone walkways, elegant topiary and untamed woods.

Jardins de Laribal

Passeig de Santa Madrona 2, 08038
Free www.barcelona.cat
Open Daily 10am–sunset
Bus 55, 150, Funicular de Montjuïc
Wheelchair access is limited due to steps and steep hills

The Laribel Gardens used to be a stone quarry and this hilly terrain was turned into a magnificent park during the Barcelona International Exposition in 1929. A series of terraces are linked by narrow roads and short paths, crisscrossed by staircases hidden among the foliage. If you're prepared to walk up the hill, you'll find gazebo pergolas surrounded by waterfalls and a pretty fountain – the Font del Gat. At different times of day the panoramas of these historic gardens change dramatically. In the evenings, you'll see the lights in the harbour lit up at dusk and if you go for a run in the morning, you'll hear birdsong as well as the booming sound of ships making their way out to sea.

Jardins de Sant Pau del Camp

Sant Pau 99, 08001
Free www.barcelona.cat
Open April–October daily 10am–9pm;
November–March daily 10am–7pm
Metro Para-lel **Bus** 21, 91, D20, H14, V11
The gardens are wheelchair accessible

A monastery dating from 911 AD used to stand on these grounds, but this modern park is a recent, quiet addition to the area. Named after the adjoining Sant Pau Del Camp church (Catalan for 'Saint Paul of the Fields'), it is a peaceful place to sit for a while after a long walk down La Rambla. It is not worth making a special visit from afar to come here, but the gardens are ideal for an impromptu picnic or a stroll in the late afternoon. Pick a spot on one of the hills and you might catch someone tending one of the handful of allotments next door.

El Jardín de Olokuti Gràcia

Carrer d'Astúries 36-38, 08012 ☎ 932 170 070
Free www.olokuti.com
Open Monday–Thursday 10am–9.30pm,
Friday–Saturday 10am–10pm
Metro Fontana **Bus** 22, 24, 39, 114, V17
There is no wheelchair access to the shop or garden

The garden at the back of this fair-trade clothes store, selling organic and ethical products made in Catalunya, is a pleasant escape from Barcelona's busy squares and thoroughfares. After browsing the range of delicate scarves and hand-crafted travelcard holders, retreat to the garden for a cup of herbal tea among the greenery.

Parc del Guinardó

Carrer Garriga i Roca 1-13, 08041
Free www.barcelona.cat
Open All day, every day
Metro Guinardó Hospital de Sant Pau **Bus** 39, 114, 117, 119
Wheelchair access is limited due to steep hills

The isolated, hilly terrain of this park make it an attractive area to go trail running (be sure to bring plenty of water, there are no cafes nearby). For those who prefer a slower pace, make your way here from the Sagrada Familia past Modernista buildings for an hour's refreshing walk with a suitably just reward. Set off early to hear the dawn chorus or amble along later for a romantic stroll at dusk.

Jardins de Turó de Puxtet

Carrer de Manacor, 08023
Free www.barcelona.cat
Open Daily 10am–sunset
Metro Vallcarca **Bus** 22, 131, H4, V15
Train El Puxtet, Pàdua
There is an accessible asphalt path running
through the park but limited wheelchair access
on the roads surrounding the gardens

Find a bench among the lush green of these
gardens and you might just spy the Sagrada
Familia and the colourful Torre Agbar in the
distance. A former stone quarry, the Sarrià-
Sant Gervasi district garden sits 178 metres
above the city, and you can now climb the hill
to the very top. Alongside palms growing on
vertiginous cliffs is an abundance of other
plants, some of which are quite rare. Look
out for the Aleppo and stone pines, acacias
and chinaberry trees as well as fan palms and
spineless yuccas. You won't find many people
walking here, so it is an exceptionally quiet
spot; strolling among the blue jasmine and
carob trees is a very calming experience.

Parc de les Aigües

Plaça Alfons el Savi 3, 08024
Free www.barcelona.cat
Open Park November–March 10am–7pm,
April–October 10am–9pm; library Monday–
Saturday 10am–2pm and 4pm–8.30pm
Metro Alfons X **Bus** 55, 92, 114, H6, V21
The gardens are wheelchair accessible

The impressive, cloudlike topiary hedges are
one of the main attractions in this pretty park
in the Horta-Guinardó district. The verdant
interior is quite hilly, and there are a number
of different terraces leading up to the summit.
It's a bit like finding your way through a maze,
as the different levels are separated by stone
walls. If you get tired of walking, or if it begins to
rain, you can always go and read a book in the
modern Biblioteca Guinardó-Merce Rodoreda on
the nearby Carrer de les Camèlies.

Places of worship

Basílica dels Sants Màrtirs Just i Pastor
Plaça de Sant Just i Pastor 1, 08002 ☎ 933 017 433
Free (Fee for access to the Bell Tower)
www.basilicasantjust.cat
Open Monday–Saturday 11am–2pm and and 5pm–8pm,
Sunday 10am–1pm
Metro Jaume I **Bus** 45, 120. V15, V17
The church is wheelchair accessible

Largely built in the 14th century, this ancient church is one of
the oldest in the city. Take some time to fully appreciate the
intricate stonemasonry, as well as the altarpiece of the Holy
Cross painted by Pere Nunyes in the Chapel of Sant Feliu. It's
also thrilling to look up at the magnificent gothic ceiling from
the centre of the nave. Next, climb up to the top of the 15th-
century campanile (octagonal belltower) for a bird's-eye view of
the buildings below. Situated in the Gothic Quarter, the Basilica
dels Sants Màrtirs Just i Pastor is quieter than other churches
in the city. It also has the added attraction of the carved stone
Fivaller fountain in the square outside.

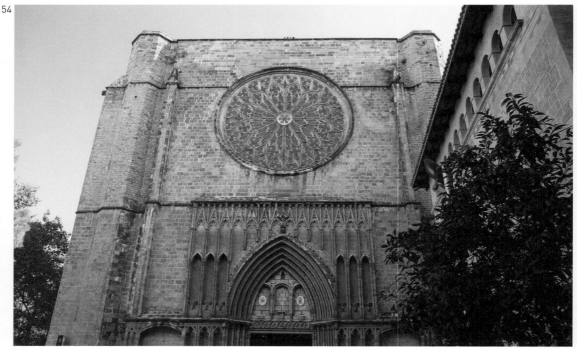

Basílica de Santa Maria del Pi

Plaça del Pi 7, 08002 ☎ 933 184 743
Free (Fee for access to the treasury and exhibitions in the crypt) www.basilicadelpi.com
Open Daily 9.30am–8.30pm
Metro Liceu **Bus** 59, 91, V13
Wheelchair users should call in advance to request a ramp to access the church

Its huge rose window, elaborate gothic entrance and extraordinary carved stonework make this church one of the architectural highlights of the city; the tall columns that form the apse are a wonder to behold. It was built between 1319 and 1391 (although the huge tower was completed a few decades later) and is a stunning example of the prevailing Catalan gothic style of the time. In winter, the candlelit interior is enchanting and the exterior just as striking when lit up at dusk. The English translation of the basílica's name is 'Mary of the Pine', one of the many names given to the Virgin, and a pine tree still grows in the square outside today.

Sant Pau del Camp

Carrer de Sant Pau 101, 08001 ☎ 934 410 001
€ (Free for service attendees) www.barcelonaturisme.com
Open Monday–Friday 9.30am–12.30pm and 3.30pm–6.30pm, Saturday 9.30am–12.30pm
Metro Paral·lel **Bus** 20, 21, 24, 64, H14
The church is wheelchair accessible

Sant Pau del Camp is an extraordinarily beautiful Romanesque church situated not far from La Rambla El Raval. Built in the 10th century by Benedectine monks, the church is the oldest in Barcelona. What makes this building particularly special are the small 13th-century cloisters; popular biblical and secular scenes have been carved into the stone columns, where you'll find etchings of lions, horses and snakes, as well as a few imaginary monsters. *Del camp* means 'of the fields', and the church used to be surrounded by orchards and meadows. Today it is surrounded by built-up streets, but it still offers some quiet respite from the hustle and bustle nearby.

Temple del Sagrat Cor de Jesús

Cimera del Tibidavo, 08035 ☎ 934 175 686
€ www.templotibidabo.es
Open Church November–February daily 11am–6pm, March–May daily 11am–7pm,
June–September daily 11 am–8 pm, October daily 11am–7pm; crypt daily 9am–8.15pm
Bus 111
The church, but not the roof, is wheelchair accessible

After a bracing walk up the mountain, this chapel is a wonderful place to rest your weary legs. Designed by Catalan architect Enric Sagnier, The Temple of the Sacred Heart of Jesus was built in the early 20th century. Although the ornate Catholic ornamentation might not be to everyone's taste, it is undeniably impressive; the chapel is famous for its huge bronze statue of Christ, which can be seen for kilometres around. The panoramic views from the roof of the chapel are also incredible, so it's well worth climbing the steep ladder to get there. However all of these attractions mean the chapel can get quite crowded, so be sure to visit just as the doors open for a more peaceful experience.

Quakers in Barcelona

Various locations ☎ 634 437 919
Free www.fwccemes.org
Open Meetings are held on the first and third Sunday of
the month at 11.30am, contact Nigel Harris on the number
above for more details

The Quakers in Barcelona are a very small group and
they don't have a permanent meeting house for their
fortnightly gatherings. However, it is not so much a fixed
meeting place that concerns Quakers, rather the peaceful
appreciation of silence in the company of like-minded
individuals. Attendees include a mixture of Catalan locals
and international visitors.

Església de Sant Felip Neri

Plaça de Sant Felip Neri 5, 08002 ☎ 933 173 116
Free www.barcelonaturisme.com
Open Monday–Friday 8am–9am, Saturday 10am–2pm
Metro Jaume I, Liceu **Bus** 14, 45, 59, 91, 120, V15, V17
The church is not wheelchair accessible

This Catholic church is typical of 16th-century
ecclesiastical architecture: a mixture of unadorned,
green-plastered walls and elaborate gold ornamentation.
The exterior walls are heavily pockmarked by an explosion
that killed 42 people – mainly infants – during the Spanish
Civil War, but today the courtyard is filled with the cheerful
sound of children's voices from the nearby school.

Shlomo Ben Adret Synagogue

Association of the medieval Jewish Quarter of Barcelona, Carrer de Marlet 5, 08006
☎ 933 170 790
€ www.calldebarcelona.org
Open Summer Monday–Friday 10.30am–6.30pm, Saturday, Sunday 10.30–2.30 pm; winter Monday–Friday 11am–5.30pm, Saturday, Sunday 11am–3pm
Metro Jaume I, Liceu **Bus** 45, 59, 120 V15 V17
There is no wheelchair access to the synagogue

Occupying a 3rd-century Roman building and turned into a space for Jewish worship – probably in the 1st century AD – this is the oldest synagogue in Europe. Now Barcelona's Historical Synagogue Museum, it is sometimes used for intimate weddings and a few other Jewish ceremonies such as Bar and Bat Mitzvahs. A tiny space, it is nonetheless full of atmosphere; Jewish people sought sanctuary here to avoid persecution during the Middle Ages. Its main purpose is the display of rare Jewish artefacts such as ornate silver dishes, a mezuzot (a parchment containing Hebrew phrases) and a precious kosher Torah from the 16th century; a guided tour around the exhibits is highly recommended.

Parròquia de Santa Anna

Carrer Santa Anna 29, 08002
☎ 933 013 576
Free (Donations welcome)
www.parroquiasantaanna.org
Open Monday–Friday 11am–2pm and 4pm–7pm,
Saturday, Sunday 11am–2pm
Metro Passeig de Gràcia, Universitat, Urquinaona
Bus 41, 42, 55, 67, 68 H15, V16
Train Catalunya
The church is wheelchair accessible

Like a number of revered churches in the Barri
Gòtic, Parròquia de Santa Anna is a pleasant
surprise hidden down a back street. Here you
can learn all about the history of the religious
order which established the church 800 years
ago. With its ancient cloisters, pretty garden and
medieval chapterhouse, it is one of the jewels of
the city. It is also the venue for occasional guitar
concerts, providing the opportunity to hear local
musicians play traditional Spanish music in an
unusual setting.

Shops and boutiques

Ganiveteria Roca

Plaça del Pi 3, 08002
☎ 933 021 241
www.ganiveteriaroca.com
Open Monday–Friday 10am–1.30pm and 4.30pm–8pm,
Saturday 10am–2pm and 5pm–8pm
Metro Jaume I, Liceu **Bus** 59, 91, V13
The shop is wheelchair accessible

Even peering through the window of this hardware shop
is exciting. Everything is immaculately displayed, from the
smallest pair of scissors to magnifying mirrors. As well
as things for the kitchen – including sturdy mandolins and
flexible steel knives for carving your *jamón ibérico* (cured ham)
– the shop stocks old-fashioned razors, badger hair brushes
and shaving soap in wooden bowls. Roca has been around
since 1911, and you'll be served by friendly staff who know
their products well. If you're looking for traditional items, this
is the best shop in town.

Casa Beethoven

La Rambla 97, 08002
☎ 933 014 826
www.casabeethoven.com
Open Monday–Tuesday, Thursday–Friday
9am–8pm, Wednesday 9am–2pm and 4pm–8pm,
Saturday 9am–2pm and 5pm–8pm
Metro Liceu **Bus** 14, 59, 91, V13
The shop is wheelchair accessible

This incredible independent shop has been
here since 1888, selling everything novice
musicians and seasoned performers could
need – customers have included some world
famous singers, including Plácido Domingo,
Montserrat Caballé and Josep Carreras,
although classical music is not the only genre
found here. Alongside sheet music and musical
instruments Casa Beethoven sells books,
CDs and recordings. On some Saturdays, live
concerts are staged – an opportunity to hear
local musicians in an intimate setting.

Sombrerería Obach

Carrer del Call 2, 08002 ☎ 933 184 094
www.sombreriaobach.es
Open Monday–Friday 10am–2pm and 4pm–8pm, Saturday 10am–2pm and 4.30pm–8pm
Metro Jaume I, Liceu **Bus** 14, 59, 91, V13
The shop is not wheelchair accessible

Occupying one of Barcelona's famed centenary buildings, this traditional hat store is a remarkable relic of the early 20th century. On passing the windows full of pale straw panamas, football caps and ladies' cotton sunhats, the interior is quite a surprise; it's altogether empty. In fact, the drawers that line the walls are full to bursting with every kind of hat you could wish for – simply ask for the model you wish to try on and, after having your head measured by a member of trained staff, your potential purchase will be retrieved. This is perhaps the closest you'll come to a living museum, but here, you can try on and buy any of the hats or caps in store.

Magatzems del Pilar

Carrer de la Boqueria 43, 08002 ☎ 933 177 984
www.magatzemsdelpilar.com
Open Monday–Saturday 10am–2pm and 4pm–8pm
Metro Jaume I, Liceu **Bus** 14, 59, 91, V13
The shop is wheelchair accessible but quite small

Ask to see one of the exquisite hand-embroidered shawls
in this shop and they will be laid out in front of you like
precious artworks. It is easy to imagine the elderly
shop assistants wearing them to church or other festive
occasions; entering this shop is like stepping back in
time. The garments make a lovely gift, or a delicate
cover-up for cooler nights on La Rambla.

La Casa de Les Sabatilles

Baixada de la Llibreteria 10, 08002 ☎ 933 150 705
www.lacasadelaszapatillas.com
Open Monday–Saturday 10.30am–2pm and 4pm–8pm
Metro Jaume I **Bus** 45, 120, V15, V17
There is a small step at the entrance

Like a number of shops in Barcelona, Sabatilles
specialises in stocking one particular item, and in this case
it's espadrilles. You can get all kinds of different designs
and sizes here, and all are still made in the traditional way
with sturdy string soles and simple canvas uppers. In
winter, come here for the comfy, natural wool slippers.

Coses de Casa

Plaça Sant Josep Oriol 5, 08002 ☎ 933 027 328
www.cosesdecasa.com
Open Monday–Saturday 10am–8pm
Metro Jaume I, Liceu **Bus** 14, 59, 91, V13
The shop is wheelchair accessible

Everything in this lovely shop is made in the upstairs atelier, from the owl-printed cushions and flowered tablecloths to plump hen keyrings, little purses and soft pillows. There are lots of nice sewn things for the kitchen here – think children's cotton aprons and brightly coloured oven mitts. This is the only place in Barcelona to buy typical Mallorcan patchwork quilts called *llengos*. Sewn from handwoven fabric in indigo blue and yellow ochre, they are a rarely seen artisanal homeware. It's hard not to feel happy surrounded by the bright oranges and crimson patterned quilts, and if they inspire you to make your own craft items, you can buy cloth by the metre here, too. To top it all, expect excellent customer service every time.

Forn de Pa Sarret Pastisseria

Carrer de Girona 73, 08009
☎ 934 874 390
www.fornsarret.com
Open Monday–Friday 7am–9pm,
Saturday 8am–2.30 pm
Metro Girona **Bus** 7, 50, 54, 62 H12
The shop is wheelchair accessible

This friendly bakery is reason enough to visit this less glamorous part of town. The 19th-century Modernista exterior echoes the traditional skills still used in the kitchen to make the countless delicious breads, cakes and bagels on offer. It was established in 1866 and the popularity of Forn Sarret shows no signs of wavering, its crusty nut breads, spelt honey loaves and chocolate croissants continuing to tempt customers through the doors. It's worth making a trip here solely for a bite of one of their divine *ensaïmada* or *crema catalana* (crème brulée).

Ferreteria Villa

Rambla de Catalunya 54, 08007 ☎ 932 160 282
www.ferreteriavilla.com **Open** Monday–Friday 9.30am–
1.30pm, Saturday 10.30am–2pm, closed on Saturdays in
August **Metro** Passeig de Gràcia **Train** Provença
Bus 7, 16, 17, 20, 22, 24, 28, 43, 44, 67, 68
The shop is wheelchair accessible

Take a little piece of Barcelona home with you via some
moulded brass door handles, finger plates and other
decorative items from this elegant ironmonger. It is
also one of the few shops where you'll find Barcelona's
distinctive, hexagonal-patterened pavement tiles – perfect
for transforming your patio.

La Pastisseria Barcelona

Carrer d'Aragó 228, 08007 ☎ 934 518 401
www.lapastisseriabarcelona.com
Open Monday–Saturday 9am–2pm and 5pm–8.30pm,
Sunday 9am–2.30pm
Metro Passeg de Gràcia, Universitat **Bus** 7, 20, 63, 67, 68
The shop is wheelchair accessible

This is a dangerous place to come if you're watching your
waistline; delicate cakes, pastries and puddings of all
colours and flavours leave customers spoilt for choice.
Each perfectly formed cake is a work of art made by
owner and 2011 world champion pastry maker José Maria
Rodríguez Guerola and his talented team of chefs.

Come In Librería Inglesa

Carrer de Balmes 129, 08008
☎ 934 531 204
www.libreriainglesa.com
Open Monday–Friday 9.30am–8.30pm, Saturday 9.30am–2pm and 4.30pm–8pm
Metro Diagonal **Bus** 7, 20, 67, 68, H10, V13, V15 **Train** Provença
The ground floor is wheelchair accessible

In the middle of the fashionable district of Eixample you'll find what is arguably Barcelona's best English book shop. There is a huge selection of popular and literary novels, as well as hundreds of paperbacks, reference books, teaching books and dictionaries, and also a good children's section. Located on a busy intersection, the shop is easy to find, but once you are inside it's quiet and peaceful. Most people come here to browse but you can also order specific books for collection.

Hibernian Books

Carrer de Montseny 17, 08012 ☎ 932 174 796
www.hibernian-books.com **Open** Monday 4pm–8.30pm,
Tuesday–Saturday 11am-8.30pm
Metro Fontana **Bus** 22, 24, 87, 114, V17
There is a small step at the entrance but otherwise the
shop is wheelchair accessible

Run by a friendly British couple, this old-fashioned book
shop contains over 40,000 secondhand books. Most of
the stock is in English although there are a few foreign
language textbooks scattered about too; it's a great
resource for teachers of English as a second language.
This is a real treasure trove for bargain hunters.

Farmacia Soler

Carrer de Jaume I 14, 08002 ☎ 933 104 226
www.farmaciafedefarma.com
Open Daily 9am–10pm
Metro Jaume I **Bus** 45, N8, V15, V17
The shop is wheelchair accessible

This well-stocked chemist is worth knowing about for a
number of reasons. It is centrally based, open every day
of the year and has late opening hours. So, whether you
need urgent precription medication or just some sun
protection cream, this is the ideal place to go. It is no
surprise that in the centre of this very walkable city, its
bestselling items are for recently acquired blisters.

Servei Estacio

Carrer d'Aragó 270-272, 08007
☎ 933 932 410
www.serveiestacio.com
Open Monday–Saturday 9am–9pm
Metro Passeig de Gràcia **Bus** 7, 20, 22, 24, 67, 68 **Train** Provença
The shop is wheelchair accessible

This large shop has almost everything you could ever need for your home and garden. From brightly coloured deckchairs (displayed on its sunny rear terrace) to artificial grass, garden spades, sewing scissors, coloured paper and cardboard gift boxes (pictured above), foam string and giant rolls of bubble wrap, it is the handyperson's heaven. A radio often plays on the sixth floor but otherwise this DIY and interior design shop is a quiet, one-stop place for anyone looking to transform their home into a stylish Catalan abode. Knowledgeable staff can help you decide which tools are right for the job and will cut everything to size, from lengths of ribbon to garden fencing.

Còpia Lab

Carrer de Sèneca 5, 08006
☎ 934 152 000
www.copialab.com
Open Monday–Friday 9am–2pm and 3.30pm–7pm
Metro Diagonal **Bus** 6, 22, 24, 33, 34, 87, V15, H8
There is a small step at the entrance but otherwise the shop is wheelchair accessible

It's difficult to decide whether this is a shop or a photo studio. In fact, it is both. Come here to pick up some analogue film and Hahnemühle fine art photography paper, or have your photos developed by a team of experienced staff. Còpia has over 25 years experience working with world-renowned photographers, and has also collaborated with museums and galleries on various exhibitions. Its list of services ranges from film scanning, image procesing and retouching, to mounting prints and framing, and its staff will also offer advice on packaging and transporting any prints you'd like to take home.

Tons Interiors

Carrer Gran de Gràcia 12, 08012
☎ 932 377 820
www.tons-interiors.com
Open Monday–Friday 10am–2pm and 4.30pm–8pm, Saturday 10am–2pm
Metro Diagonal **Bus** 6, 22, 24, 33, 34, 87, H8, V15
There is a small step at the entrance but otherwise the shop is wheelchair accessible

After stepping into this sophisticated interior design shop you may never want to leave; soft mohair blankets drape gracefully over solid oak chairs, capacious sofas come covered in fabrics made from all natural fibres, and pale, semi-translucent linen curtains hang from the ceiling. The colour scheme is muted, with largely dove-grey and monochrome furnishings, and hand-crafted ceramics such as Rina Menardi's exquisite matt black bowls complete the picture. The grey velvet cushions are the shop's own designs, as are the coffee tables and iron shelving units.

Cereria Subira

Baixada de la Llibreteria 7, 08002
☎ 933 152 606
www.cereriasubira.net
Open Monday–Thursday 9.30am–1.30pm and 4pm–8pm, Friday 9.30am–8pm, Saturday 10am–8pm
Metro Barceloneta, Jaume I **Bus** 45, 120, V15, V17
There is a large step at the entrance so wheelchair access may be difficult

The interior of this shop is almost as fascinating as its eclectic collection of candles. A black and white chequered floor leads to a grand curving staircase and a backdrop of pastel-coloured wall panels: a suitable setting for the display of sophisticated chandeliers and simple beeswax candles. From huge church candles pierced with incense, to tiny red- and white-spotted toadstools and kitsch cartoon figures, you will find all kind of wax wonders in this extraordinary shop. This is the ideal place to come if you are looking for a unique, impeccably-packaged gift.

Laie

Carrer de Pau Claris 85, 08010
☎ 933 181 739
www.laie.es
Open Monday–Friday 9am–9pm, Saturday 10am–9pm
Metro Passeig de Gràcia, Plaça Catalunya, Urquinaona **Bus** 7, 22, 28, 39, 45, 50, 54, 56, 62 B20, B24
The shop is not wheelchair accessible

It is easy to find a recently published Spanish language book here, whatever your desired genre; cinema, theatre, literary theory, poetry, gastronomy and art and architecture are just some of the topics accounted for. As well as novels and a wide range of non-fiction for both adults and children, Laie has an excellent selection of coffee table books on art and design, alongside monographs on the Spanish masters Gaudí and Picasso. It's spread over 300m², so you're bound to find a quiet corner to browse a few titles. Once you're done reading, you can retreat to the cafe on the mezzanine level.

Natural Mediterrani

Carrer d'Astúries 33, 08012 ☎ 934 159 682
www.naturalmediterrani.com
Open Monday–Saturday 10.30am–2.15pm
and 5pm–8.30pm
Metro Fontana **Bus** 22, 24, 39, 114, V17
There are small steps at the shop entrance, but
assistance with wheelchairs can be provided

The majority of the organic beauty products in this shop
come from the Catalan or Aragon regions. Plant-based
ingredients and a low carbon footprint make this an
attractive store for the environmentally conscious, and a
welcome change from the high-street cosmetic counters.

Dolceria de la Colmena

Plaça de l'Àngel 12, 08002 ☎ 933 151 356
www.pastisserialacolmena.com
Open Daily 9am–9pm
Metro Jaume I **Bus** 45, 120, V15, V 17
There is a small step at the entrance but otherwise the
shop is wheelchair accessible

Roughly translating as 'The Sweet Shop', the Dolceria is
a must-visit for anyone after a sugar-coated biscuit to
dip in their morning coffee. Nougat and other sweets line
the shelves, and all are beautifully wrapped. Don't leave
without trying a slice of the Xixona nougat mousse cake.

Markets

Sunday Flea Market

Carrer del Portal de Santa Madrona 22, 08001
www.fleamarketbcn.com
Open Every second Sunday 9am–4pm (weather dependant)
Metro Drassanes **Bus** 21, 88, H14, V11
There is good wheelchair access to the stalls

You're sure to find a few nice surprises at this unpretentious
fortnightly flea market in the El Poble-Sec district (between
La Rambla and the Maritime Museum). Vendors pitch up to
sell and recycle old goods, from skinny rib jumpers and warm
duck-down jackets to beautiful old Spanish peseta notes
and classic posters. The women's clothes tend to be quite
small, but there is a huge variety of other items to browse and
everything comes at a bargain price.

Mercat de la Llibertat

Plaça de la Llibertat 27, 08012 ☎ 932 170 995
www.mercatsbcn.com
Open Monday–Friday 8am–8.30pm, Saturday 8am–3pm
Metro or **Train** Fontana **Bus** 22, 24, 87, 114, V17
There is good wheelchair access and facilities

The heritage building home to the Mercat de la Llibertat
is worth a visit in itself. Built in the 1880s, it has been
sensitively modernised and is now a colourful space in
which to do your food shop. Your basket will be full of
fantastic Spanish products in no time, so take advantage
of the home delivery service if you find you can't carry
everything back to the kitchen.

Feria de Alimentos Artesanales

Plaça del Pi, 08002
www.oldbcn.com
Open First and third Friday, Saturday and Sunday of every
month 10am–9pm **Metro** Jaume I, Liceu **Bus** 59, 91, V13
The market is wheelchair accessible

Run by the Colectivo de Artesanos de la Alimentaciòn
and overlooked by the Santa Maria del Pi cathedral, this
friendly organic market stocks all manner of groceries.
Fill your larder with wild mushrooms picked from the
surrounding hills and sweet jams made with apricots or
bitter oranges. Less crowded than the Boqueria indoor
market, it's an altogether calmer shopping experience.

Mercat dels Encants

Carrer Castillejos 158, 08013
☎ 932 463 030
www.encantsbcn.com
Open Monday, Wednesday, Friday–Saturday 9am–8pm
Metro or **Tram** Gloriès **Bus** 62
The market is wheelchair accessible

If you get tired of the noisy hawkers that parade the beach on sunny days, seek some welcome shade at this nearby flea market. Although the prices are not the cheapest in the city, the atmosphere is lively and the building worth a visit for anyone with an interest in urban architecture. As well as a lot of vintage pieces gleaned from attics and grandparents' glass cabinets, there's a fair deal of uninspiring mass-produced items. But as with most markets of this kind, the serendipity of finding something you didn't expect is what makes it exciting. The market can get very busy, so come early for a more peaceful shopping experience.

Places to relax

Aire Barcelona

Passeig de Picasso 22, 08003
☎ 932 955 743
€ www.airedebarcelona.com
Open Daily 9am–10.30pm
Metro Jaume I **Bus** 39, 51, H14 **Train** Estació de França
There is good wheelchair access to the pools and
massage area

The first Aire baths opened in Seville in 2008 and it is easy to
see why they have become so popular. This Barcelona spa is
housed in a magnificent old building that used to be a former
meat storage area in the El Born Market, full of ancient
wells that supplied the city with water. The building has been
carefully renovated and the brick vaults removed to create
the *banos Arabes* (Arabic baths) you find here today. From the
moment you step through the huge front door, you know you
are somewhere special – softly lit lamps and the sound of
trickling water welcome you as you enter the reception area,
and the soothing atmosphere continues into the main room
where candles emit a warm, romantic glow. If you can, try
and spend at least three hours here to make the most of the
different baths and various treatments available – after a rest
in the frigidarium, try the caldarium, a hot steamy hammam,
or book a relaxing argan oil massage.

Yoga Body

Carrer de Roger de Flor 118, 08013

☎ 932 991 379

€ www.yogabody.es

Open Monday–Friday 10am–10pm, Saturday, Sunday 10am–3pm (check the website for specific class times)

Metro Tetuan **Bus** 6, 7, 19, 50, 51, 55, 62, H12

The studio is wheelchair accessible, call in advance to check suitability for each class

This innovative yoga company has three separate studios in Barcelona, but in the modern Roger de Flor branch you can take classes in yoga trapeze. The gravity-defying exercises, performed as you hang upside down from a large loop of orange cotton, can be incredibly soothing. The focus here isn't so much on the spiritual side of yoga, but more on the physical benefits. There are no mantras, chanting or Sanskrit terms used in the classes, but the multilingual teachers do also run workshops on meditation, breathing and nutrition.

Flotarium

Plaça Narcís Oller 3, 08006 ☎ 932 173 637
€ www.flotarium.com
Open Monday–Saturday 10am–9pm
Metro Diagonal **Bus** 6, 33, 34 H8, V15 **Train** Gràcia
Call ahead for help and advice about wheelchair access

There are few quicker ways to become totally relaxed
than floating in a warm bath in a small, soundproof
cocoon – you don't even have to know how to swim.
Described by regulars as *una sensacio unica* ('a unique
sensation'), floating in warm water for 50 minutes
provides the opportunity to completely forget the outside
world and reconnect with yourself.

Aqua Urban Spa

Carrer Gran de Gràcia 7, 08012 ☎ 932 384 160
€ www.aqua-urbanspa.com **Open** Monday–Sunday
9.30am–9pm **Metro** Diagonal **Bus** 6, 33, 34, H8, V15, V17
Aside from the vitality pool, the spa is wheelchair accessible

Inspired by the city's Roman baths, this massage centre
is an excellent place in which to truly wind down. Sit
quietly in the Finnish sauna, take a dip in the small
thermal pool or stretch out on one of the loungers covered
in pearl-coloured mosaic tiles. As a special treat, you can
book a reflexology or aromatherapy session, or if you're
feeling indulgent, a warm chocolate facial – a particularly
luxurious way to slow down in this quiet, urban spa.

Silom Spa

Carrer de València 304, 08009 ☎ 932 726 662
€ www.silomspa.com
Open Monday–Saturday 10.30am–9.30pm
Metro Girona, Passeig de Gràcia **Bus** 39, 45, 47, V17
Steps at the entrance make wheelchair access difficult

This is the only authentic Thai spa in Barcelona and
on arrival you'll notice a few Thai Buddhas glowing
in the candlelight under a curved teracotta tiled roof.
Treatments include bamboo therapy sessions as well
as other more conventional holistic treatments for both
physical and mental complaints. Whichever you choose,
you are sure to leave feeling lifted and energised.

Spa Zenter Hotel Grums

Carrer de Palaudàries 26, 08004 ☎ 934 420 666
€ www.hotelgrumsbarcelona.com
Open Daily 11am–9pm
Metro Paral-lel **Bus** 20, 21, 64, 121
There is limited wheelchair access to the spa

This small but pristine spa at the bottom of La Rambla is
ideal for all seasons. In winter, have a languorous dip in
the hot tub, and on warmer days bring a bathing suit and
float for a while in the tiny pool. The powerful jets of water
are particularly effective at massaging sore shoulders – a
fantastic way to banish jet lag or general weariness after
a long day at work.

YHI Wellness Spa

at Meliá Barcelona Sky, Avinguda de Sarrià 50, 08029
☎ 933 672 050
€ www.melia.com
Open Daily 11am–9pm
Metro Entença, Hospital Clinic **Bus** H8 27, 32, 41, 59
Aside from the spa bath, the hotel is wheelchair accessible

Perhaps because it is a bit out of the centre, this large, international hotel feels less hectic than others. Call ahead to book a session in its small spa and you will be pampered and cared for like nowhere else. The wellness area feels private and secluded, and discreet lighting creates an intimate atmosphere. It is very easy to lose track of time here; with just a gentle massage the pressures of everyday life simply melt away.

Massage & Beauty Salon La Rambla

La Rambla de Sant Josep 75, 08002
☎ 653 317 553 or 931 405 463
€ www.massagebarcelona.net
Open Daily 2.30pm–9pm
Metro Liceu **Bus** 59, 91, V13
The salon is not wheelchair accessible

The 30-minute back or foot massages on offer in this salon come highly recommended by travellers – they're inexpensive and you don't have to book an appointment in advance. Each masseuse receives at least six months' training in 'kilo massages', a powerful technique that removes knots and muscle tension. You can also ask for depilation sessions and a few other beauty treatments here. The interior may not be the most sophisticated but the staff are friendly and for a central Barcelona location, the price is excellent.

OrVita Teràpies

Carrer de Ferlandina 24, 08001
☎ 640 123 492 or 930 171 331
€ www.orvitaterapies.es
Open Monday 4.30pm–8.30pm, Tuesday–
Saturday 10am–2pm and 4.30pm–8.30pm
Metro Sant Antoni, Universitat
Bus 24, 41, 55, 91, 120, H16
The beauty centre is wheelchair accessible
and has adapted toilet facilities

Formerly a large warehouse space, the unusual
premises at Orvita date from 1847. Lovingly
restored, the ancient fireplaces and original
fittings have been kept intact to form an
interesting backdrop to this eco-conscious spa.
One of Barcelona's best centres for alternative
and holistic therapies, it has been practising
for over 10 years. The amiable staff will make
you feel right at home as well as give you expert
advice on the best vegetarian- and vegan-based
products to use on your skin.

Places by water

Banys del Fòrum
Carrer de la Pau 12, 08930 ☎ 932 210 348
Free www.barcelonaturisme.com
Open July-September daily 11am–2pm
Metro or **Tram** El Maresme/Forum **Bus** 7, 143, H16
The bathing area has adapted toilet and changing room facilities and a hydraulic chair for people with disabilities to access the water

If you fancy a dip in the sea without getting sand in your shoes and sandwiches, make a beeline for the bathing area in the Parc del Fòrum. It's halfway between a beach and an indoor pool; shallow steps lead from a paved sundeck down into the Mediterranean sea. Sit on the edge of the concrete ledge and dangle your legs in the cooling seawater, or immerse yourself completely via one of the stepladders. The swimming area is shallow and trained volunteers are on hand to assist bathers with reduced mobility. A green flag will also indicate whether or not it is safe to swim.

Jardins del Príncep de Girona
Carrer de Taxdirt, 08025
Free www.barcelona.cat
Open Daily 10am–dusk
Metro Alfons X, Sant Paul Dos de Maig **Bus** 92, V21
The park is wheelchair accessible

Close to the port, these gardens are a good place to rest after a walking tour of the city. Seek some shade from the midday sun under the leafy trees or rest on one of the stone benches next to the large pond; it's a charming spot to simply sit and do nothing. However, if you feel a bit more energetic there are also ping-pong tables in one corner – bring your own bats and balls. Sometimes live music is played here and the cafe can get lively in the evenings but otherwise it is a tranquil spot.

Pont Elevat
Port Fòrum, Carrer de la Pau 12, 08930
☎ 933 562 720
Free www.barcelona.cat
Open All day, every day
Metro Sant Martí, Poble Nou **Bus** 7, 36, H14, H16 **Tram** Forùm
The bridge is wheelchair accessible

Not least due to its impressive architecture, Barcelona's harbour is an interesting place to wander around. Stroll along the jetty past large luxurious yachts and shiny white boats and cross the Pont Elevat (pictured above) towards the Mediterranean Sea. There are some stunning vistas from here: in one direction sit dignified 18th-century houses, the Diagonal Mar shopping mall and the many factories that line the River Besòs, and in the other stretches the deep blue sea. There are also a few cafes dotted along the water's edge – ideal for a jug of chilled sangria on a hot summer's day.

Piscina Municipal de Montjuïc

Avinguda de Miramar 31, 08038

☎ 934 430 046

€ www.picornell.cat

Open End of June–early September 11am–6.30pm (days and times vary so call ahead before visiting)

Metro Para-lel **Bus** 55, 150, Funicular de Montjuïc

The pools are not wheelchair accessible

On hot summer days when the beach gets a little too crowded, come up to this collection of outdoor swimming pools on Montjuïc Hill. The complex was built in 1929 for the Olympic Games and professional swimmers often come here to practise their strokes. Open to people of any age and ability, it is a very reasonably priced way to cool off - take a look over your shoulder while on the diving board and you'll also be treated to a unique view of the city below.

Grand Hotel Central SkyBar
Via Laietana 30, 08003
☎ 932 957 900
€ www.grandhotelcentral.com
Open April-October daily 9pm–1am, exclusive access to guests prior to 9pm
Metro Jaume I **Bus** 45, 120, V15, V17
There is good wheelchair access to the rooftop pool

For a truly memorable evening among the roofs of Barcelona, book a table at the Grand Hotel Central's SkyBar. Reserved for guests during the day, the roof terrace of this prestigious establishment incorporates a crystal-clear infinity pool and a classy restaurant that opens to the public from 9pm. Take a quick dip before dinner or simply sip on a cocktail while admiring the view – undoubtedly the best you'll find in this part of town.

Confraria de Pescadors de Barcelona
Lugar Moll del Rellotge 54, 08039
☎ 932 217 745
Free www.confrariapescadorsbarcelona.com
Open Daily auctions at 7am and 4.45pm
Bus 88
The fish market is wheelchair accessible, but the floor can get very wet and slippery

For freshly caught fish straight off the boat, arrive at this fish market bright and early. Restaurant chefs from all over the city come here to pick up mackerel, hake, whiting and more to make up their dish of the day. The market is also a great place to pick up boquerones, squid, red shrimp, octopus and the ever-popular sardines. On the website for the Fishermen's Association is a calendar showing which species of fish are caught each month: a handy tool to help you plan your meals for the week in advance.

Parc de la Ciutadella

Passeig de Picasso 21, 08003 ☎ 638 237 115
Free www.barcelonaturisme.com
Open December–February daily 10am–6pm;
March and November daily 10am–7pm;
April–October daily 10am–8pm
Metro or **Tram** Ciutadella/Villa Olímpica **Bus** 120
The park is wheelchair accessible

This varied, leafy inner-city park is well loved
by locals. Families come here to push babies in
prams, play with toddlers and amble along the
paths. It can get busy by the Three Dragon Castle
but there are a few quiet spots. On sunny days
you will find at least one person sitting in the
shade of a tree reading a book, undisturbed by
the families emerging from the zoo. The most
peaceful pastime here is rowing on the lake –
rent a small boat and enjoy the calm of a
summer afternoon on the water.

Galleries

Galeria ADN

Carrer d'Enric Granados 49, 08008
☎ 934 510 064
Free www.adngaleria.com
Open Monday 3pm–8pm, Tuesday–Friday 10am–2pm and
4pm–8pm, Saturday 11am–2pm and 5pm–8.30pm
Metro or **Train** Provença **Bus** 20, H10
The gallery has a small step at the entrance but is otherwise
wheelchair accessible

This is one of the few galleries in Barcelona to show work
with a conceptual bias and it has built up a solid reputation for
thought-provoking installations and socially conscious projects.
Foreign Office (2015) by Moroccan-French artist Bouchra Khalili,
for example, combined powerful video footage and sobering
photographs to document the offices of various organisations
across Algiers involved in the liberation movements of 1962 to
1972. In contrast to traditional documentaries of this nature,
Khalili's reflections on this period of history border on poetic.
Cultural, historical and political issues are often at the forefront
of exhibitions here, and the images consistently salient as
a result. The name ADN tranlates to DNA in English and,
fittingly, this gallery forms an integral component of this city's
artistic makeup. Don't miss it.

Galeria Carles Taché

Carrer de Mèxic 19, 08004
☎ 934 878 836
Free www.carlestache.com
Open Tuesday–Friday 11am–2pm and 3pm–8pm
Metro or **Train** Plaça Espanya **Bus** 13, 23, 150
The gallery is wheelchair accessible

This award-winning gallery has been curating interesting projects with artists and a number of innovative institutions for more than 25 years. Carles Taché, the owner, teaches on the MA course at Barcelona University so there is almost guaranteed to be intelligent, groundbreaking work on display whenever you visit. Exhibits have included a one-person show by French artist Adriana Wallis that comprised simple photographic portraits alongside burnt paper drawings and curious glass sculptures – you never quite know what you'll see next. Nevertheless it's a very acccessible gallery, one devoted to the appreciation of art, as can be seen by its large collection of art publications.

Sala Parés and Galeria Trama

Carrer Petritxol 5, 08002 ☎ 933 187 020
Free www.salapares.com
Open Tuesday–Friday 10.30am–2pm and 4pm–8pm, Saturday 10.30am–2pm and 4.30pm–8.30pm,
Sunday (October–June only) 11.30am–2pm
Metro Liceu **Bus** 14, 59
There is wheelchair access to the ground floor but not the Gallery Trama on the upper floor

The Sala Parés gallery is one of the most prestigious in Barcelona, having been around since 1877. It has an illustrious history and many internationally renowned artists, such as Pablo Picasso and Francesco Goya, have shown here. Downstairs you'll find mainly figurative and representational paintings, such as landscapes and still lifes by Glòria Muñoz and vivid watercolours by Francesc Artigau. Upstairs, however, is an entirely different story – this floor is home to Galeria Trama. Here you'll come across more modern, experimental pieces, often large photographic works and colourful abstract paintings. In this unique space there is truly something for everyone.

3 Punts Galeria

Carrer d'Enric Granados 21, 08007
☎ 934 512 348
Free www.3punts.com
Open Monday 4pm–8pm,
Tuesday–Saturday 11am–8pm
Metro Passeig de Gràcia, Universitat
Bus 54, 58, 64, 66, 67, 68, V15
The gallery is wheelchair accessible

3 Punts has occupied a spot on this charming, semi-pedestrianised street for the last couple of years, but has been a key player on Barcelona's art scene since 1994. It has always been a keen supporter of Spanish artists, so the images and figurines on display have been remarkably consistent over the decades. The work of Gerard Mas has been exhibited here a number of times, and his traditional busts with a mischeivous twist are always popular. Samuel Salcedo's life-sized, three-dimensional portraits with rabbit ears are similarly playful, while the carved wooden sculptures by Efraïm Rodríguez are astonishing, both for their verisimilitude and their often unnerving exploration of the female body. The gallery is included on the Contemporary Art Route, an annual event to encourage people to visit contemporary art galleries in the city.

Artur Ramon

Carrer de la Palla 25, 08002
☎ 933 025 970
Free www.arturamon.com
Open Monday 5pm–8pm, Tuesday–Friday
10am–1.30pm and 5pm–8pm, Saturday
10am–1.30pm
Metro Jaume I, Liceu **Bus** 51, 91, 120, V1, V13
The gallery is wheelchair accessible

Wandering through the many rooms of this extraordinary antique dealer is like walking through a wonderful museum, except here everything is for sale, from animal skulls covered in pearls and coins to paintings by Antoni Tapiès. It really is an entrancing wunderkammer, not least thanks to the midnight-blue paint on the walls, which lends each room the air of an entrancing grotto filled with precious jewels. The Ramon family have been here for four generations, and are world experts on antique artefacts as well as contemporary art. Look out for the intricate yet sinister glass sculptures by Yolanda Tabanera and the 13th-century crucifix featuring a gold-painted loincloth. The gallery also features photo-realist memento mori and vanitas still life paintings by Josep and Pere Santilari.

etHALL

Carrer de Joaquín Costa 30, 08001 ☎ 606 802 323
Free www.ethall.net
Open Monday–Friday 11am–2pm and 5.30pm–9pm, Saturday 11am–2pm
Metro Sant Antoni, Universitat **Bus** 24, 41, 55, 64, 91,120, H16
There is a step at the entrance and the gallery is small but otherwise wheelchair accessible

If you wander down the narrow back streets of the Gothic Quarter, you'll come across this interesting gallery displaying contemporary drawings. One of the few European art galleries to specialise in works on paper, this is an excellent space to discover Spanish artists. The director shows a mixture of abstract and figurative pieces, from line drawings to comic books. At the back of the gallery is another small exhibition space selling and promoting artists' books. Here you'll find some unusual limited-edition works made by artists from around the world. They tend to be conceptual rather than illustrated editions, but it is hard to leave without purchasing an affordable, beautifully produced publication.

Nogueras Blanchard

L'Hospitalet de Llobregat, Carrer Isaac Peral 7, 08902 ☎ 934 636 313
Free www.noguerasblanchard.com
Open Monday–Friday 10.30am–7pm, closed during August
Metro Santa Eulalia **Bus** L16, L52, L82, L85
The gallery is not wheelchair accessible

Located in an industrial district of the city, this gallery has enough room to initiate some ambitious and groundbreaking projects. Having recently moved to the new 540-square-metre venue in l'Hospitalet de Llobregat, the Nogueras Blanchard programme focuses on conceptual works, with artists often working in interdisciplinary mediums. The gallery invites younger curators to propose work for the space, making this a democratic and exciting location for contemporary collaborations, and also runs a series of kitchen talks where artists, critics, curators and those interested in art and culture are invited in for informal interviews and discussions.

Galeria Joan Gaspar

Plaça del Dr Letamendi 1, 08007 ☎ 933 230 748
Free www.galeriajoangaspar.com
Open Monday 5pm–8pm, Tuesday–Friday 10.30am–1.30pm and 5pm–8pm, Saturday 10.30am–1.30pm
Metro Passeig de Gràcia, Universitat **Bus** 7, 20, 50, 54, 66, 67, 68, H 10, H12
The gallery is not wheelchair accessible

Starting life as the the Sala Gaspar in 1909, this is one of the longest-standing galleries in Spain. A wide range of work is on display here including Francisco Goya's extraordinary etchings from the *Los Capricos* series. Having promoted work by Pablo Picasso, Salvador Dalí, Antoni Tàpies and other world-renowned artists in its early days, Joan Gaspar now selects work by younger painters and sculptors such as Ruth Morán, whose cosmological abstract paintings *Diagnosis e infinito* were perfectly suited for this unusual space. The gallery building is interesting in itself and won an architecture prize in the 1970s. An aluminium-framed wooden door and unusual interior angles make this a quirky yet sophisticated venue for some astounding contemporary art.

Ana Mas Projects
L'Hospitalet de Llobregat, Carrer Isaac Peral 7, 08902 ☎ 936 337 475
Free www.anamasprojects.com
Open Monday–Friday 11am–7pm, Saturday by appointment
Metro Santa Eulalia **Bus** L52, L82, L85, LH2
The gallery is not wheelchair accessible

Ana Mas Gallery has been based in Barcelona for the past 13 years and recently opened a second branch in San Juan, Puerto Rico. Having moved into a larger space in L'Hospitalet, the gallery programme has been divided between both spaces, giving more room to show work by some remarkable artists. Here you might see installations and publishing projects as well as drawings and conceptual work. Most of the artists on display are Spanish, and past exhibitors have included Carmen Mariscal, Xavier Miserachs, Alberto Peral, Àngels Ribé, Soledad Sevilla and Ana Tiscornia. Don't be deterred by the industrial-looking exterior; the work here is cutting edge, often site responsive, and immersive.

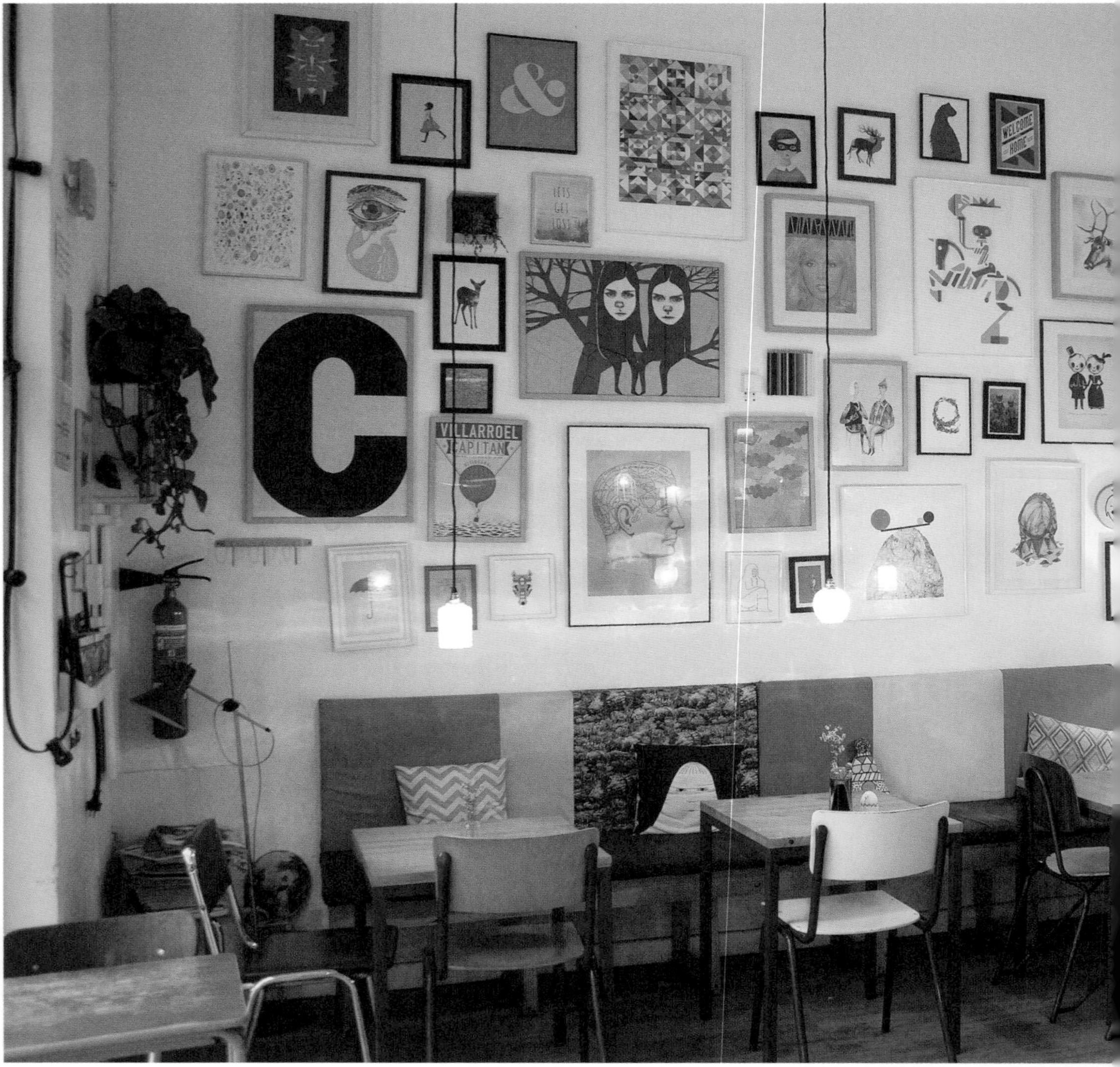
&
WELCOME
HOME
C
VILLARROEL
CAPITAN

Cafes and bodegas

Café Cometa

Carrer del Parlament 20, 08015 ☎ 930 073 203
www.cafecometa.com
Open Monday–Wednesday 9am–10pm, Thursday 9am–11pm,
Friday–Saturday 10am–midnight, Sunday 10am–10pm
Metro Poble Sec **Bus** 37, 121
The cafe is wheelchair accessible with adapted toilet facilities

Housed in a former industrial building, this light and airy cafe
is the type of place you'll want to sit for hours doing nothing
much at all. If you're after some light reading, grab one of
the many newspapers, books or magazines dotted around to
flick through while you sip on your coffee, or simply sit back
and admire the original prints and paintings on the walls. The
menu is simple but varied with a mixture of fish and meat-
based dishes as well as vegetarian and vegan options; the
friendly staff are able to accommodate every dietary need. The
lemon cupcakes and manzana apple cakes – a Swedish recipe
made with vanilla, orange and cinnamon – are divine.

Miscelanea

Carrer de Guàrdia 10, 08001 ☎ 933 179 398
www.miscelanea.info
Open Wednesday, Thursday, Sunday 5pm–11pm, Friday–Saturday 5pm–2am
Metro Drassanes **Bus** 59, 91, 120, V13
The cafe is not wheelchair accessible

This versatile space is more than just a cafe, it's also an art gallery and cultural hub. Emerging artists and illustrators from around the world show their work here, and pieces vary from light-hearted drawings and sketches to handmade illustrated books. You might also hear some experimental music playing somewhere in the building. As well as your daily coffee fix, you can order fluffy cakes, colourful salads and freshly squeezed juices, and if you want to linger for a while there are newspapers and books lying around that you are free to browse. Before you leave, pick up an unusual gift and support up-and-coming Catalan artists in the process.

Väcka

Carrer de Sèneca 4, 08006 ☎ 930 188 769
www.vacka.weebly.com
Open Monday midday–8pm, Tuesday–Thursday 9am–8pm
Metro Diagonal **Bus** 6, 33, 34, V15 **Train** Gràcia
The cafe is wheelchair accessible but quite small

This raw food and vegan cafe makes healthy eating less of a chore and much more of a pleasure; with dairy-free banana and nut waffles and chocolate and strawberry puddings on the menu there's still the opportunity to indulge, but here you can do so guilt-free. All the food is made fresh on site and you can take away a Väcka picnic to enjoy al fresco on one of the benches outside. If you don't mind the music playing inside, the interior is a clean, bright space decorated with floating air plants in delicate glass baubles.

Cafè de la Pedrera

Casa Mila, Passeig de Gràcia 92, 08008 ☎ 934 880 176
www.lapedrera.com
Open daily 8.30am–midnight
Metro Diagonal **Bus** 7, 16, 17, 22, 24
Train Passeig de Gràcia, Provença de la Pedrera
The cafe is wheelchair accessible

The undulating ceiling, sinuous windows and bright white interior of Gaudi's Casa Milà make it one of Barcelona's most interesting restaurants, but also a favourite among tourists. Come here in the early morning to dodge the crowds and enjoy a tortilla and cortado in peace.

El Cafè de La Central

Mallorca 237, 08008 ☎ 935 504 643 or 934 875 018
www.lacentral.com/web/librerias/cafeteria
Open Tuesday–Saturday 10am–9pm
Metro Diagonal, Provença **Bus** 7, 67, 68
The building is wheelchair accessible

The Central Bookshop Cafe is tucked away on the first floor of a smart, well-designed bookshop. At the rear of the shop on the first floor you'll find tables and chairs and a balcony with a lovely view over the garden. Located on the edge of the Eixample district, it's a great place to linger on a quiet afternoon, and it is easy to find an unobtrusive corner to read in with a cup of coffee in hand.

Bodega la Palma

Carrer de la Palma de Sant Just 7, 08002 ☎ 933 150 656
www.bodegalapalma.com
Open Monday–Friday 9am–midnight, Saturday midday–midnight
Metro Jaume I **Bus** 45, 120, V15, V17
There is a small step at the entrance but otherwise the bodega is wheelchair accessible

Recommended by locals who know the area well, this is not only the oldest bar in Barcelona but also one of the most atmospheric. Evolving from a humble grocers in the 1930s, when you could drop by and fill your empty bottles with as much wine or olive oil as you needed, it has now become one of the most characterful bars in the city. It's a haunt of artists, writers and filmmakers, and the looming arches and large wooden barrels of this go-to destination make it a charming spot to meet up with friends for some tasty Catalan food and a *cerveza* (beer) or glass of port. Tapas is king here, and the chorizo and fried potatoes a must-try.

Cafè d'Estiu

Museu Frederic Marès, Plaça Sant Lu 5-6, 08002 ☎ 933 103 014
www.cafedestiu.com
Open November–March Tuesday–Saturday 10am–7pm, Sunday 11am–8pm;
April–October Tuesday–Sunday 10am–10pm **Metro** Jaume I **Bus** 45, V15, V17
Wheelchair access is limited due to the steps at the entrance to the museum

This cafe is tucked inside the Museu Frederic Marès, one of the quaintest museums in the city. With its wooden walls, woven cane roof over the counter and blooming bougainvillea, it feels like a rural getaway in the middle of the city – just a stone's throw from the Barcelona Cathedral. Residents count it as one of their favourite spots for lunch or a light supper outdoors, and globally inspired plates draw on Spanish, Turkish and South American cuisine. On a warm sunny day, order a bowl of guacamole with nachos or enjoy a fresh mint tea with bread and hummus while leafing through one of the magazines you'll find on the table by the bar.

Casa Vives

Rambla de Catalunya 58, 08007 ☎ 932 160 269
www.casavives.com
Open Monday–Saturday 8am–9pm, Sunday 9am–3pm
Metro or **Train** Passeig de Gràcia **Bus** 7, 50, 54, H12
There is a small step at the entrance to the cafe and patisserie

A small cafe and patisserie, Casa Vives bakes some exceptional cakes and crafts its own handmade chocolates. Presented on the cafe's pristine white tables, the dark Madagascan chocolate cake looks particularly delectable. Pop down to purchase some edible gifts, or merely if you fancy a sit down and a cup of tea. A range of herbal teas are available – mint (*menta poleo*), chamomile (*manzanilla*) and lime flower (*til-la*) among them – or opt for a freshly squeezed, ice-cold orange pressé on a hot day. Casa Vives is also one of the few places in Barcelona you can order *horchata*, a delicious dairy-free drink made from tiger nuts. On your way out you might also want to pick up a packet of delicious soft almond nougat, known locally as *torrons*.

Plantaciones de Origen

Carrer Gran de Gràcia 193, 08012 ☎ 932 177 447
Open Daily 7.30am–9pm
Metro Fontana **Bus** 22, 24, 39, 87, 114, V17
There are steps up to the front door and the toilet

Not only a cafe, Plantaciones is also an importer of coffee beans. As you enter, you'll see large sacks of coffee, sourced from all around the world, waiting to be ground. The specialist shop doesn't just serve espressos, though – you can also sip gunpowder tea or an unusual white leaf brew. It's a bit quieter at the back, where you can sit underneath a typical Catalan terracotta tiled ceiling.

Bar Bodega Quimet

Carrer de Vic 23, 08006 ☎ 932 184 189
Open Monday–Friday 10am–11pm, Saturday, Sunday midday–5pm and 6pm–11pm
Metro Fontana **Bus** 22, 24, 87 **Train** Gràcia
There is wheelchair access but no adapted toilet facilities

This traditional wine bodega has been renovated with great care by two young brothers and has managed to retain some of its original atmosphere. Order tapas dishes such as grilled octopus, *patatas bravas* (cubed potatoes in a tomato sauce) and squid cooked in its own ink alongside a glass of cava. The quietest time to visit is during the week at midday or in the late afternoon.

Bodega Bonavista

Carrer de Bonavista 10, 08012 ☎ 932 188 199
Open Monday–Friday 10am–2.30pm and 5pm–9pm, Saturday midday–3pm and 6pm–9pm, Sunday midday–3pm
Metro Diagonal **Bus** 6, 33, 34
The bodega is wheelchair accessible

If you are wandering around Gràcia and fancy a drink in a local bar, be sure to seek out this delightful bodega. Once inside you can order a glass from an excellent selection of wines, which provide the perfect accompaniment to the regional cheeses on offer. *Bodega* means 'cellar' or 'wine bar' and the multilingual bartenders are very knowledgeable, so a visit here provides a great opportunity to learn about Catalan wines and regional cured hams. Although the bar often plays jazz in the background, it is small and comfortable enough to make you feel quite at home.

Restaurants

La Cassola
Sant Sever 3, 08002 ☎ 933 181 580
Open Monday–Wednesday 9am–4pm,
Thursday–Friday 9am–4pm and 8pm–11pm
Metro Sant Jaume, Liceu
Bus 45, 59, 120, V13, V15, V17
There is wheelchair access but no adapted toilet facilities

Run by four hardworking sisters, the atmospheric Cassola
has been serving up classic Catalan dishes for more than 20
years. It's music-free and cosy, and you can choose to dine
at street level or in the old cellar below. Typical main courses
might include salt cod with a garlic mousse or Catalan
sausage stuffed with mushrooms. Unfortunately vegetarians
are not well catered for, but a cream of celery soup might be
a perfect winter dish for a non-meat eater at lunchtime. A
few Catalan newspapers are available for lone diners, who are
very welcome in this friendly, hospitable restaurant.

Restaurant Torre de Alta Mar

Passeig de Joan de Borbó 88, 08039 ☎ 932 210 007
www.torredealtamar.com **Open** Sunday–Monday
8pm–11.30pm, Tuesday–Saturday 1pm–3.30pm and
8pm–11.30pm **Metro** Barceloneta **Bus** 39, V15
The restaurant is wheelchair accessible

There are a number of restaurants overlooking the sea
here, but this is the only one situated at the top of an
iron tower. Its unusual location and panoramic views of
the city, alongside a simple and sophisticated interior,
make for an attractive dinner destination. The food is also
excellent – as with many restaurants on the port, seafood
is king. Opt for the prawn risotto or bluefish Catalan stew.

Neri Restaurant

Sant Sever 5, 08002 ☎ 933 177 442
www.hotelneri.com
Open Daily 7.30am–11am, 1.30pm–4pm and 8.30pm–11pm
Metro Jaume I, Liceu **Bus** 45, 91, 120, V15, V17
There is a steep step at the entrance to the restaurant

This elegant restaurant can be found on the ground floor
of the sophisticated Neri Hotel. Loud music is played
indoors though, so if possible choose a seat in the quiet
square opposite the church. The food is good, but tends to
come in smaller portions so order a few dishes if you feel
hungry. The black rice lobster risotto is lovely – follow it
up with a passion fruit and white chocolate eclair.

Manairó Restaurant

Carrer de la Diputació 424, 08013 ☎ 932 310 057
www.manairo.com
Open Monday–Saturday 1.30pm–3.30pm and 8.30pm–11pm
Metro Monumental **Bus** 7, 405, 614, 640, 643, 648, H12
There is a small step at the entrance to the restaurant

Typical fare at Michelin-starred Manairó includes French mackerel *à la meunière* (breaded mackerel fillets with a butter and parsley sauce), seafood gazpacho, squid broth with onions and pork with mashed beans. Although meat and fish dishes dominate the menu, you'll find the occasional vegetarian dish such as fried pizza with gorgonzola and truffles. The chefs seem to enjoy experimenting with unusual ingredients and combinations of flavours here, as can be seen in the pumpkin and carrot caked served with sweet orange sorbet. The restaurant is particularly special at night, when diners are directed towards their tables by candlelight – a very romantic setting for a meal before a trip to the nearby National Catalan Theatre.

Afrodita

Carrer d'en Carabassa 3, 08002 ☎ 931 770 769
Open Daily 1pm–midnight
Metro Liceu, Drassanes **Bus** 45, 120, V15, V17
The restaurant is wheelchair accessible (call
ahead to request the ramp) but has no adapted
toilet facilities

Next to Plaça de George Orwell, this small,
friendly restaurant has a lovely outdoor terrace.
Highly recommended by locals, Afrodita offers
great food at reasonable prices. It's described
as having a creative Asian/Mediterranean
menu, so you'll find some really tasty dishes
including burgers with rustic potatoes and
the signature Afrodita salad, with avocado,
rocket, strawberries, figs, pine nuts and mini
mozzarella balls. Close to Barcelona Cathedral
but far enough away from the crowds on La
Rambla, this is a good place to drop by after
a few hours walking around the city. The
restaurant occasionally plays bossa nova
music, but it is quieter outdoors.

Gut Restaurant

Carrer del Perill 13, 08012 ☎ 931 866 360
www.restaurantgut.com
Open Monday–Thursday 1pm–4pm and
7pm–11pm, Friday–Saturday 1pm–4pm
and 7pm-midnight
Metro Diagonal, Verdaguer **Bus** 6, 33, 34, H8
The restaurant is wheelchair accessible but has
no adapted toilet facilities

Despite its location in a trendy, up-and-coming
area, this is a surprisingly unassuming place
to eat. The decor is sparse but homely and
the service is attentive and friendly. But it is
the food that is the star attraction here. It
draws on traditonal Catalan cuisine but with
a modern twist, so you never quite know what
delicacies might appear on your plate. The
delicious *bacalao* (shredded cod) salad is a
treat, as is the thinly sliced seared beef and new
potatoes served on a simple grey slate. There
are numerous gluten-free and vegan dishes as
well, and the chefs seem to be able to cater for
anyone. The restaurant starts the evening by
playing background music but this fades away
as more diners appear. During Gracia Festival
Week in mid-August you can reserve a table
in the street to soak up the friendly, festive
atmosphere in the open air.

La Mar Salada

Passeig de Joan de Borbó 59, 08003

☎ 932 212 127 or 932 211 015

www.lamarsalada.cat

Open Monday–Friday 1pm–4pm and 8pm–11pm, Saturday, Sunday 1pm–11pm

Metro Barceloneta **Bus** 45, 59, D20

The restaurant is wheelchair accessible

This charming portside restaurant offers a real taste of the Mediterranean. Albert and Maria started La Mar Salada ten years ago and the family business has become well known for its high-quality food – Albert used to be a pastry cook at the famous Oriol Balaguer and their chef, Marc Singla, used to work at the prestigious Talaia with the celebrated Ferran Adrià. The inexpensive three-course menu changes every week according to season and the fish is bought straight off the boats each morning. Despite playing soft music, it retains a restful atmosphere and provides a welcome alternative to the tourist traps nearby.

Iaia Cristina

Carrer de la Llacuna 22, 08005 ☎ 934 617 311
Open Monday–Thursday 7am–11.30pm, Friday 7am–1am,
Saturday 8am–1am, Sunday 8am–midnight
Metro Llacuna, Poble Nou **Bus** 6, 26, 36
The restaurant is wheelchair accessible but has no
adapted toilet facilities

Iaia means 'grandma' in Catalan and the owner of this
airy, modern restaurant is justly proud of his traditional
family cooking. If you have a liking for gnocchi, Iaia serve
it in a deliciously rich tomato-basil sauce. Near to a few
chain hotels, this is a quiet corner in a part of town where
tourists tend not to linger. They are missing a treat.

Casa Amalia

Passatge del Mercat 4–6, 08009 ☎ 934 589 458
www.casamaliabcn.com
Open Tuesday–Saturday 1pm–3.30pm and 9pm–10.30pm,
Sunday 1pm–3.30pm
Metro Girona **Bus** 7, 50, 54, 62, H12, H10, B24, 39, 45, 47, V17
There are steps at the entrance to the restaurant

Right next to Mercat de La Concepció, this down-to-earth
eatery is the ideal spot for a hearty lunch after a morning
of shopping. The restaurant has an à la carte menu that
includes gazpacho, hake with mushrooms, seafood paella
and *esqueixada de bacalao* (a traditional Catalan dish of
shredded cod with olive oil, tomatoes and onions).

Places to sit and walk

Jardins de Rubió i Lluch

Carrer de l'Hospital 56, 08001 ☎ 933 020 797
Free www.barcelona.cat
Open November–March daily 10am–7pm;
April–October daily 10am–9pm
Metro Liceu **Bus** 91, 120
The garden is wheelchair accessible

Sometimes hard to find on city maps, these lovely gardens are hidden behind tall, formidable walls. Once inside, however, they are a haven of calm. Enter by the Passatge de l'Hospital or, at the other end, Carrer de l'Hospital and you'll find yourself surrounded by ancient brick buildings that house, among other institutions, the renowned Biblioteca Sant Pau-Santa Creu. Art students wander in and out of the Escola Massana Art School where anyone can apply to take one of the vocational training courses, which range from mural design to textile art.

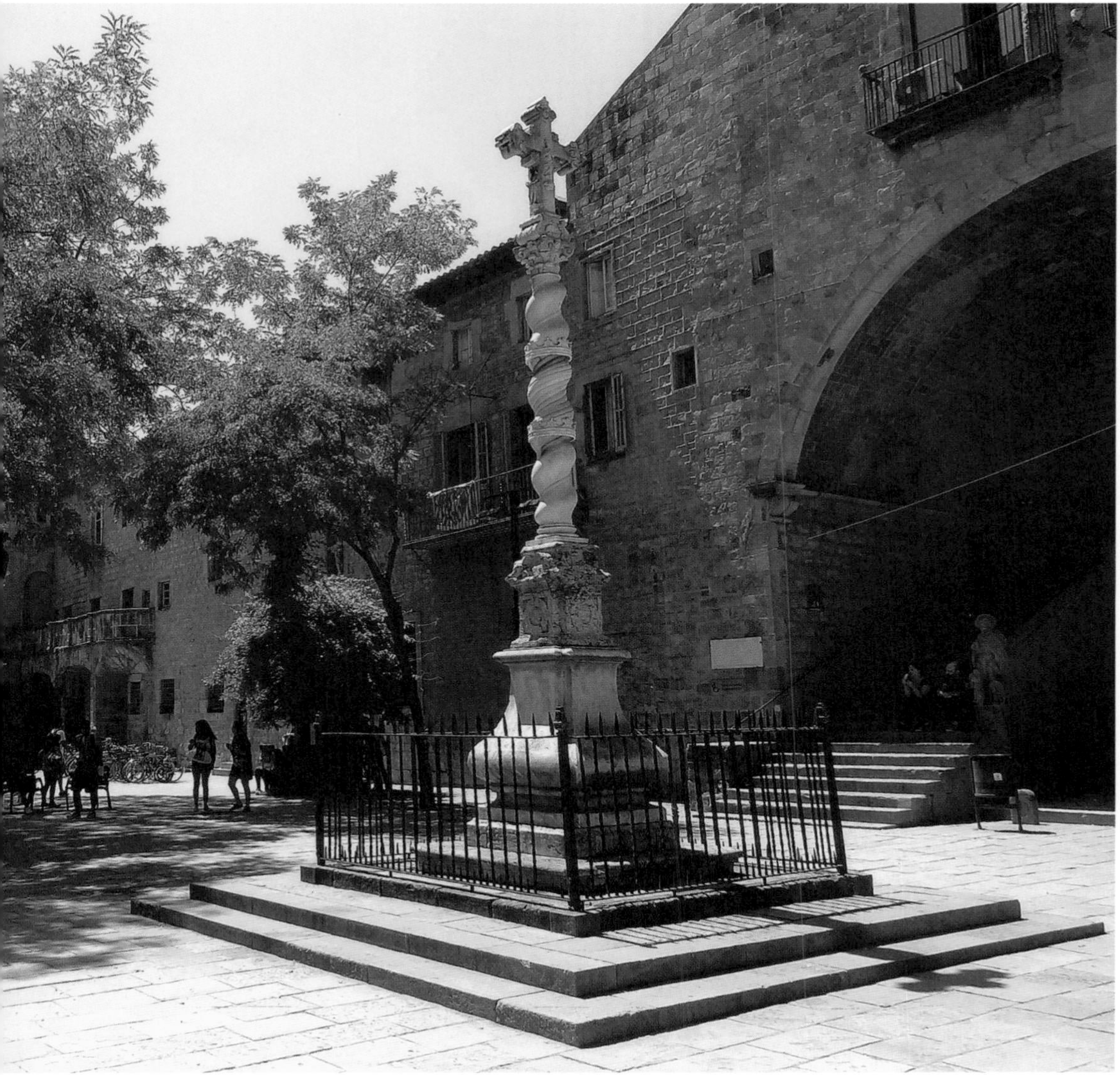

Catedral Basílica Metropolitana de Barcelona

Plaça de la Seu s/n, 08002 ☎ 933 428 262
Free (Fee to access the roof of the cathedral)
www.catedralbcn.org
Open Cloister Monday–Saturday 8.30am–
12.30pm and 5.45pm–7pm, Sunday 8.30am–1pm
and 5.15pm–7pm
Metro Jaume I **Bus** 45, V15, V17
There is wheelchair access to the cloister, and
to the cathedral via the Door of Saint Eulalia
(Carrer del Bisbe)

Nestled within this 15th-century cathedral is
an enchanting cloister that provides a peaceful
place to linger in the otherwise crowded Gothic
Quarter. Unusually, it is home to 13 white geese
– kept here as a reminder of the age at which
Saint Eulalia was martyred. The four walls of
the cloister surround a large pond (Font de les
Oques) and palm trees and orange trees provide
shelter from the sun. Look up for a glimpse of
the cathedral roof and its impressive gargoyles,
carved in the shape of both mythical and
familiar creatures.

Cementiri de Poblenou
Avinguda d'Icària, 08005 ☎ 932 251 661
Free www.cbsa.cat/cementiri-poblenou
Open Daily 8am–6pm
Metro Llacuna **Bus** 14, 26, 36, 41
The cemetery is wheelchair accessible

Tall palm trees and stone benches greet you
at the entrance to this small cemetery just a
couple of metro stops outside the city centre.
You'll also find a small group of cypress trees;
in Greek mythology this species is associated
with mortality and the underworld. Once inside
the cemetery however the greenery is restricted
to a few faded flowers pinned to the memorial
plaques that line the walls. If you want to
discover another side to Catalan family history,
this is an interesting place to visit.

Bunker del Carmel

Carrer del Turó de la Rovira, 08032
Free www.museuhistoria.bcn.cat/ca/node/16
Open All day, every day
Metro Guinardó/Hospital de Sant Pau, El Coll/La Teixonera **Bus** 24, 92, 119, V17
The roads are steep here and the area quite hilly, so wheelchair access may be difficult

A visit to a collection of abandoned anti-aircraft bunkers may not sound inspiring, but in fact this is a wonderful, secluded and often deserted area. Overlooking Parc del Guinardó, these derelict monuments are a fascinating mix of crumbling concrete and pristine Mediterranean forest. Built during the Spanish Civil War to protect the city from bombing, the bunkers are now part of the MUHBA (Museu d'Història de Barcelona), although have been neglected long enough to have acquired their own anti-aesthetic charm. It's a relatively trendy location now, but remains a lovely spot for people looking to appreciate the solitude and awe-inspiring 360-degree views of the surrounding area.

Torre de Collserola

Carretera de Vallvidrera al Tibidabo s/n, 08017 ☎ 934 069 354
€ www.torredecollserola.com
Open See website calendar for dates and times
Bus 111
The tower is wheelchair accessible

Getting to this spot is quite the adventure. From Plaça Catalunya take the funicular to Vallvidrera Inferior, walk to Valvidrera Superior and then take the bus three stops to Cruïlla de Carreteres – from there, the spectacular Torre de Collserola is three minutes' walk away. The journey is well worth your while. From the top of this prize-winning Norman Foster-designed telecommunications tower you can see the Mediterranean Sea stretching far into the distance, as well as major landmarks such as Gaudí's Sagrada Familia. On hot summer days, it's cooler up on this hill than on the beach and it also offers some respite from the crowded streets below. If you're a keen photograper it's a must – even after dark, the sight of the glittering city below is simply stunning.

Avinguda de Gaudí
Avinguda de Gaudí, 08025
Free www.barcelonaturisme.com **Open** All day, every day
Metro Sant Pau/Dos de Maig, Sagrada Familia **Bus** 19, 20, 45, 47, 92, H8, V21
The pavements are wheelchair accessible

This avenue cuts diagonally across the Eixample district connecting the remarkable Sant Pau Art complex by Domènech i Montaner at one end (see page 29) with the stunning Sagrada Familia at the other (both worth a visit). The street is largely pedestrianised and has two cycle lanes, which makes it much less noisy than other thoroughfares. A number of cafes have also set up outdoor seating areas along the central corridor, so it is easy to find somewhere to stop and have a drink if you decide to walk from one end to the other. Look out for the elegant Modernista streetlamps which give the street its distinctive character. Designed by Pere Falqués, they were placed along the Avinguda de Gaudí in 1985 after being stored for many years in a warehouse. Come here in the early morning when it is quieter, as the area gets busy as the day progresses.

Cine Verdi

Carrer de Torrijos 14, 08012 ☎ 932 387 990
€ www.cines-verdi.com/barcelona
Open See website for screening times
Metro Fontana, Joanic **Bus** 39, 114
Four of the cinema screens are wheelchair accessible

This lovely old-fashioned cinema tends to show Spanish-language, independent, European and old black-and-white films, alongside the occasional Hollywood blockbuster. It's a great spot for cinephiles and anyone who is looking for a cosy, intellectually stimulating place to spend an evening during the winter months. The bar is also a nice place to sit and chat about everything cinematic.

Parc del Centre del Poblenou

Avinguda Diagonal 130, 08018
Free www.barcelonaturisme.com
Open December–February daily 10am–6pm; March, November daily 10am–7pm; April, October daily 10am–8pm; May–September daily 10am–9pm **Metro** Poblenou **Bus** 7, 40, 42, B20, B25, V7 **Train** Pere IV, Fluvià
The park is wheelchair accessible

French architect Jean Nouvel was invited to redesign this neglected site in Diagonal Mar, and he created a stunning piece of contemporary garden design. Irrigated by groundwater and maintained using sustainable technologies, it is a lush green, modern urban oasis.

Terrace at Museu Nacional d'Art de Catalunya

Palau Nacional, Carrer del Mirador del Palau Nacional s/n, 08038 ☎ 936 220 360
Free (Fee for access to the museum) www.mnac.cat
Open Terrace November–February Sunday–Thursday 10am–7pm, Friday–Saturday 10am–9pm; March, April, October daily 10am–9pm; May–September Monday–Wednesday 10am–8pm, Thursday–Sunday 10am–midnight
Metro or **Train** Plaça Espanya **Bus** 13, 37, 55, 150, Funicular de Montjuïc
Most of the building and terrace is wheelchair accessible

Originally built for the International Exhibition of 1929, the National Palace of Montjuïc is now home to the National Museum of Catalan Art, and its terrace is a spacious sun trap. Surrounded by palm trees and complete with its own urban waterfall, it's the perfect place in which to sit and watch the world go by. The museum itself is full of medieval treasures, as well as some extraordinary landscape paintings by Marià Pidelaserra. If you like the great master's work, an entire room is dedicated to the Catalan Modernista designs of Gaudi and his protégé Josep Maria Jujol.

Castell de Montjuïc

Carretera de Montjuïc 66, 08038 ☎ 932 564 440
€ (Free for children and on Sundays after 3pm) www.barcelona.cat
Open November–March 10am–6pm; April–October 10am–8pm
Metro Paral-lel then Funicular de Montjuïc **Bus** 150
The fortress is not currently wheelchair accessible

This very solid fortress on the top of Montjuïc Hill has a notorious history. Perched on the highest point in the area, it was originally built as a watchtower, before it was extended in the 17th century to become a castle. The military then used the stronghold to suppress civil riots in the 18th and 19th centuries, and after the end of the Spanish Civil War it was turned into a prison. You can visit the courtyard where prisoners were allowed to exercise, as well as the former cells. Now, it is a peaceful location with gorgeous views of the harbour below. It is also set to become a Centre for Interpretation, where visitors can learn about the geology of Montjuïc Hill as well as the history of the inhabitants of the surrounding area, from early setters to modern day residents.

Teleferico del Puerto
Avinguda Miramar s/n, 08038 ☎ 934 304 716
€ www.telefericodebarcelona.com
Open Summer 11am–8pm; winter 11am–5pm
Metro Para-lel **Bus** 21, 121
The cable cars are wheelchair accessible

For dramatic views of the Mediterranean from a quiet
vantage point, these aerial cable cars are just the ticket.
The short trip might seem expensive, but if you walk up
the hill beforehand you'll feel you deserve ten minutes
sitting down in an old-fashioned cable car. If you ascend
from the port, you'll find some pretty gardens to wander
through as you exit the car on top of the hill.

Plaça de les Glòries Catalanes
Gran Via de les Corts Catalanes s/n, 08013
Free www.barcelonaturisme.com
Open All day, every day
Metro Glòries **Bus** 7, H12
The square is wheelchair accessible

Plaça de les Glòries is an unusual public space with an
abundance of astounding contemporary architecture. On
sunny days the paved square is full of portable furniture
free for anyone to use. There are even three chairs with
USB connections and built-in solar panels should you
wish to charge your camera, and a mobile library loans
books, board games and other activities.

Rambla del Poblenou

between Passeig de Calvell and Carrer de Tànger, 08005 **Free**
Open All day, every day
Metro Llacuna, Poblenou **Bus** 6, H16, N7, V27
The Rambla is wheelchair accessible

If you prefer to spend your evenings in a calmer, more relaxed part of town, ignore La Rambla in the centre and catch a bus or tram to the Rambla del Poblenou in the north-east of the city. This lovely street is full of independent shops and cafes with outdoor terraces where locals linger over a coffee or a beer until the early hours of the morning. People amble rather than rush here, and the almost traffic-free street has its own warm, unpretentious character. This is the sort of place you could spend hours hopping from one bar or restaurant to another. Try chatting to locals if you want to practise your Spanish or Catalan, and then sample some local delicacies from an authentic tapas bar.

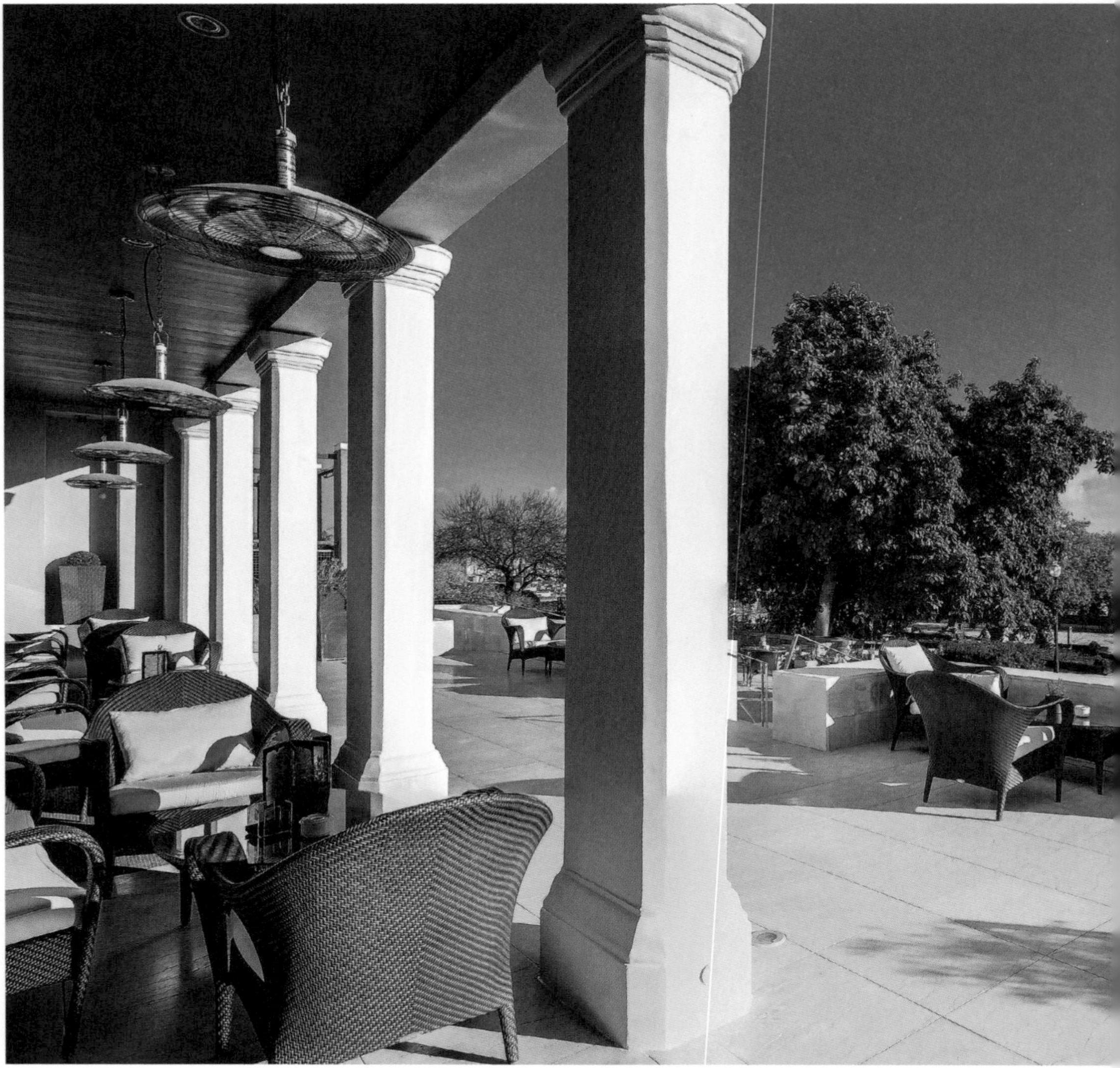

Places to stay

Hotel Miramar

Plaça de Carlos Ibáñez 3, 08038
☎ 932 811 600
www.hotelmiramarbarcelona.com
Bus 55, 150, Funicular Miramar
There is good wheelchair access in the hotel and two
specially adapted bedrooms

This large hotel on top of the Montjuïc Hill has spectacular
views of the city, and is a wonderful place to retire to after a
day of exploring the tourist sites below. Surrounded by the
Laribel Gardens – planted with Mediterranean pines, tall
cypresses, loquat and fig trees and huge palms – it feels quite
rural on this side of the mountain. Built in the 1920s, the hotel
used to be a palace, and it still retains some of its former
opulence. Not only is there an indoor spa with a sauna and
treatment rooms, but also an outdoor pool with accompanying
Balinese lounge beds. This is undoubtedly the quietest part
of the hotel, especially in the mornings before everyone has
woken up – lie down and unwind amid the chirping of the
birds (and the occasional deep boom of ships coming into the
harbour, a gentle reminder that this is still a maritime city).

Circa 1905

Carrer de Provença 286, 08008 ☎ 935 056 960
www.circa1905.com
Metro Diagonal **Bus** 6, 33, 34 **Train** Provença
The hotel is not wheelchair accessible

This beautiful building dates from the 1850s
and many of the original features have been
retained in a classy renovation. The interior is
exquisite – both the bedrooms (each with its
own colour scheme) and living area are full of
old prints and antiques dating from the period of
the building's construction, and the rear rooms
look out on to a lovely garden. The atmosphere
is warm and the staff welcoming, and perhaps
the only problem you might encounter is finding
it hard to leave once you have arrived. Gentle
music is sometimes played in the salon, but the
bedrooms and the rear of the hotel are generally
very peaceful.

Happy Apartments

Carrer Nou de la Rambla 10, 08001 ☎ 618 222 099
www.happyapartmentsbarcelona.com
Metro Drassanes, Liceu **Bus** 59, 91, V13
There is a lift but rooms cannot accommodate a wheelchair

These well-equipped city centre apartments are light
and spacious. Designed with pristine white walls and
tasteful furnishings, they are pleasant suites in which to
relax and recuperate. With both two- and three-bedroom
apartments available, they are suitable for both familes
and groups of friends. More personal than a hotel, a stay
here will feel both special and stress free.

Angla Luxury Apartments

Carrer de València 290, 08007 ☎ 656 851 405
www.anglaboutiqueapartments.com
Metro Passeig de Gràcia **Bus** 22, 24, 39, 45, V17
There is wheelchair access but no adapted bathrooms

Angla Luxury Apartments offer some of the best
apartments in the city, whether in Eixample or near to the
Passeig de Gràcia. Ideal for couples, friends or families,
the stylish rooms are immaculate and comfortable.
The apartments in Carrer València are close to some
fashionable boutiques, interesting museums and chic
Catalan restaurants, but you'll find your apartment is a
haven of peace from the lively streets outside.

Casa Camper
Carrer Elisabets 11, 08001
☎ 933 426 280
www.casacamper.com
Metro Liceu, Universitat **Bus** 14, 59, 120 **Train** Catalunya
There is a lift and one room with an adapted bathroom for wheelchair users

Casa Camper Hotel is quite different to others you will find in the city. Each room incorporates an attractive chillout space (if you book into a suite, this comes in the form of an entirely separate lounge area) and the roof terrace has a refreshing outdoor shower – ideal in hot weather. In the lobby you can help yourself to tasty sandwiches, yoghurts, chilled water and cups of tea, all included in the price of your room. Such perks have made this hotel popular among travellers and it can often get busy, so take advantage of the comfortable sofas in your personal relaxation space. And if you'd also like a break from the hubbub of the streets outside, request a room with windows on to the lush green vertical garden (pictured above).

Hotel Ilunion
Carrer de Ramòn Turró 196-198, 08005
☎ 932 438 800
www.ilunionbarcelona.com
Metro Llacuna **Bus** 6, 26, 36
The hotel has a number of wheelchair accessible rooms

This four-star hotel might look like any other found in large cities but it has a very different philosophy. Not only are there are a number of rooms fully accessible for wheelchair users, but there are also braille signs in the lift and a hoist to enable people with physical impairments to enter the small rooftop pool. In addition, the hotel actively welcomes people with disabilities to apply for work there; this progressive policy ensures everyone feels welcome. The roof terrace is a lovely, quiet place to relax, and the rooms are well soundproofed. It's the perfect place to stay if you'd like a large, quiet room not too far from the centre of town.

Gran Hotel La Florida

Carretera de Vallvidrera al Tibidabo 83–93, 08035
☎ 932 593 000
www.hotellaflorida.com
Bus 111
The hotel is wheelchair accessible

This five-star hotel is located far from the city centre but it's worth staying here for the peaceful location and excellent spa. It's not as difficult to get to as it initially seems – bus services into the mountains surrounding Barcelona make it possible to reach without a car. The interior of the hotel is traditional with a contemporary twist, and the grey velvet upholstered sofas are both lovely to look at and tempting to sit on. The main reason to book a stay here, though, is to sample the treatments in the wonderful spa, particularly after a long walk in the surrounding hills. Be sure to climb the steps of the Camì de la Font del Bacallà to the Bacallà Spring, a constantly flowing fountain of water emerging from a carved stone plaque in the mountainside.

Index of places by area